Don't Be Scared LIVE ON PURPOSE!

WRITE YOUR DESTINY STATEMENT™ AND LIVE THE LIFE OF YOUR DREAMS

Omar M. Barlow and Jéneen Nicole Barlow
Foreword by Dr. Willie Jolley

Barlow Enterprises
Philadelphia, PA

Library of Congress Cataloging-in-Publication Date is available.

Cover and Interior Designs by BJ Cook, ™

Author photograph by Tiana G. Anderson, Ubara Photography

Legal Disclaimer
While none of the stories in this book are fabricated, some of the names and details may have been changed to avoid embarrassing or invading the privacy of the individuals mentioned.

Although the author and publisher have made every effort to ensure that the information in this book was correct at press time, the author and publisher do not assume and hereby disclaim any liability to any party for any loss, damage, or disruption caused by errors or omissions, whether such errors or omissions result from negligence, accident, or any other cause.

Contents

To Corrine

may this book bless you! Live on purpose!

We dedicate this book to you. May you live full of passion, hope, sincerity and zeal.

May you unapologetically fulfill your reason for being and may you have a ridiculous amount of fun in the process.

Serve your generation well, Destiny Seeker.

And die empty.

DOWNLOAD YOUR FREE GIFT!

Just to say ***THANK YOU*** for downloading our book, we would like to give you this Special Report Absolutely FREE!

"The Four Pillars of Purpose: A Philosophy for Purposeful Living." You can access it right now at:

www.destinystatement.com

"There is nothing noble in being superior to your fellow man; true nobility is being superior to your former self."

~ Ernest Hemingway

Foreword by Dr. Willie Jolley

"The minute you make a decision and move in a new direction is the minute you change your life! You might not reach your destination in a minute but you can certainly change your direction in a minute…and in that minute you change your life!"

-- Taken from *It Only Takes a Minute To Change Your Life* by Dr. Willie Jolley

This is a piece that I have shared countless times in my travels as I speak, train, and motivate people all over this world. And today, I specifically want to share it with you because this speaks to how the minute you picked up this book and start reading it, could be a minute that changes your life. I encourage you to keep reading and you will see why I am so excited about this work.

Every now and then you come upon people who uplift you by their presence and their thinking, and you can sense greatness just by being with them. That is what I experienced when I met Omar and Jéneen Barlow.

It was my pleasure to get to know both Omar and Jéneen Barlow at my Speaking Business Bootcamp. It was immediately clear that they were both dynamic presenters, who were not just interested in making a dollar, but in making a difference!

I've continued to develop a relationship with them. They listen, they probe and they ask penetrating questions. The Barlows consistently think through the critical issues, and when they implement, they move forward with a spirit of excellence!

This book exemplifies that spirit of excellence. This is the second in their "*Don't Be Scared*" book series. In this book, *Don't Be Scared. Live on Purpose!* Omar & Jéneen provide you with the inspiration and information necessary to overcome your fears, so you too can take action on your dreams and make them into realities. They provide the clarity you need so you can take precise actions that will change your life forever.

Don't Be Scared. Live on Purpose! is filled with timeless principles, moving stories, and practical steps for living an intentional life!

I recommend you read this book, re-read it, then share it with your friends and family members. If you take this action, you will understand why I say this minute can change your life, because the person who picked up this book will not be the same person who puts it down at the completion of the reading.

I am confident that you will make stellar strides toward mastering how to live a life of meaning, simplicity and joy. I promise, regardless of what setbacks you may have experienced, by reading *Don't Be Scared. Live on Purpose!* you just set yourself up for one of your most significant comebacks of all.

Dr. Willie Jolley,* Hall of Fame Speaker, Syndicated Radio Show Host and Author of The Best Selling Books: *It Only Takes A Minute To Change Your Life* and *A Setback Is A Setup For A Comeback!

REVIEWS

This is really such a great book. *Don't Be Scared. Live on Purpose!* will help people who are living purposeless and meaningless lives. If you are confused about the real meaning and purpose of your life then this book will help you. This book will equip you to *think about your life* and it will move you towards making your dreams come into reality. This is one of the most encouraging books I have ever read.

Lako Lama
Minister
Pokhara, Nepal

Reading *Don't Be Scared. Live on Purpose!* was life-giving. I was excited to learn, with specific guidance, how to be my best self. The things that I have been searching for or missing in my life, this book laid out for me. Now I feel empowered and equipped to become my best self and to live my best life. I greatly appreciate Jéneen's and Omar's transparency. I can relate to them. They make me feel confident and the way the book read made me eager to keep reading and to complete the Destiny Seeker Challenges. I loved the exercises. The Barlows have created a clear process that showed me that I too can Live on Purpose. If you are lost, tired of doing things the same or just bored with life, then read *Don't Be Scared. Live on Purpose!* and you will have a life changing experience. Thank you Jéneen and Omar for allowing God to use you to inspire and equip lives *on purpose.*

Towanda Tilson, MSW, M.Div
Chester, PA

Omar and Jéneen Barlow are aligned with their purpose. They flow in their River of Destiny, as individuals and as a couple. I love their statement, "Be a Student of YOU!" *Don't be Scared. Live on Purpose!* will give you the "Deep Dive" You've been seeking and show you how to Work, Love, Live and Be More Excellent."

Dr. Cheryl Adams, Founder
Heart to Heart Connections
Middletown, DE

This book will be a great asset to my clients. I can't wait to share it with the young women I work with. The step-by-step process is user friendly and will hold folks accountable; so practical too.

Robyn J. Murphy, President
Further Her Consulting Group
Philadelphia, PA

Don't Be Scared. Live on Purpose! holds the secret that educational systems don't want you to think about. One of the things that strikes me most is how the book reminds us not to let our schooling interfere with our education. Life never stops teaching us and this book expounds in detail on how to get the most of your existence!

Kayon Watson
Fundraising Coordinator
New York, NY

Hello! We are Omar and Jéneen Barlow, and for nearly 15 years we have had the joy and honor of giving people the process and assistance they need to produce tangible, long-lasting results in their businesses and in their lives.

Too few people truly love the work they do! Yet there *are* an exceptional few whose work brings joy and energy to their lives every single day. What makes these brilliant few so different from the masses around the globe who are unfulfilled with their life and work?

Recent Gallup Poll studies indicate that nearly 90% of the world's workers say that they are unhappy and unproductive. So, only 10% of people in the world find joy and significance from what they do for over half of their waking hours every single day?

This is an epidemic that needs a solution!

Maybe you've invested much of your energy, money and time into creating a successful career for yourself. Many of us teach our children to do the same and we invest even more energy, money, and time into helping them to make "success" happen for themselves.

To make matters more challenging, in our society, the demands of excelling at work, and in life in general, seem to require never-ending sacrifice. Knowing this, it should be your highest priority to ensure that you and your loved ones do not fall into the elusive, joy-robbing trap of becoming successful at doing the wrong thing.

What's your thing – really?

A very sharp gentleman who was an Executive Partner of ours comes to mind.

Raphael was a very successful professional in one of the top three most lucrative industries in the world. He'd trained with the world-renowned peak performance coach, Mr. Anthony Robbins, and had even successfully mastered Robbins' fire-walks. Raphael had studied and trained with hosts of others who are among the very best in the industry of personal development. Simply put, this gentleman was an elite professional who highly valued personal development. Raphael hired us as his personal coaches and began the Destiny Statement™ process because he had come to a place, as many successful people do, at which he needed to *reassess* his life and what his next steps should be.

After just three, very productive sessions, Raphael said that he was "*rejuvenated.*" He said that he was dreaming audaciously again. He had remembered, and begun to work towards, making some of his deepest heart's desires happen. I (Jéneen) noticed that Raphael's voice was alive again. He actually sounded like a new man.

Raphael felt trapped because he was a great "success" at something that he did not love. He was thriving in his industry but he ***really*** wanted to be a philanthropist, a public speaker, and an author who told the stories and lessons he learned from interviewing elite athletes.

Raphael's story is one of many. Remember, the research affirms that almost 90% of people in the world, do not find joy in what they do each day. The exact research reports that of the 230,000 people in 142 countries around the world who responded, that 86% of them are "high dissatisfied" with the work they do. In America, only 1% claimed that the "love their work."

Despite what fame, money, or accolades you accumulate, research and history consistently confirm that becoming a success in the wrong field *always* leads to nothing more than a life of gross un-fulfillment and depressing discontent.

If you could take one, easy, quick action that would immediately give you more joy, clarity, peace, and excitement about your life and work while also making you feel much more fulfilled and on purpose, wouldn't you do it?

So, what does it take to banish fear and Live on Purpose?

In *Don't Be Scared. Live on Purpose!* we reveal to you the exact, inspiring, easy, proven way to quickly escape the unclear, unhappy 90% of the world's workers.

We show you exactly where to begin so that you can push past the fear of pursuing your passion and instead take your rightful place among the most productive, happy, 10% of people around the world -- because that winning circle *is* exactly where you belong.

Using compelling, funny, heart-warming stories of struggle and success and the Destiny Statement™ Process that we created and have taught to thousands of men, women, and children internationally for over 15 years, this book solves the issue of workplace discontentment by teaching you 4 must-have principles for purposeful living.

Most importantly, *Don't Be Scared. Live on Purpose!* gives you an easy to follow blueprint for figuring out what on earth you were born to do.

When you are finished reading this book, you will know what you love to do and for whom. You will graduate far beyond the elementary, vague, "I just love helping people," answer to the question "What do you love to do?" to a sharp, crystal clear, unflinchingly confident statement of who you are, what you do, and for whom. This advanced self-knowledge will empower you!

Even better, it positions you to pursue and get paid to do your life's work instead of merely being a paid professional at something that you may or may not be great at, but that you do not love.

This book is for people who suffer from feeling "all over the place" and for people who are tired of pretending that they are content.

It is also for people who have no clue what to major in at their college or university.

It is the magic bullet for leaders who need help to motivate, inspire and increase productivity, morale, and teamwork among their staff.

It is for insightful people who sense that, in spite of their successes or failures to date, there is something else -- ***something more*** -- that they want and need to do with their lives.

If you are fed up with hearing and reading about purpose focused lives and purpose driven work, then this book is for you!

If you're tired of being motivated and inspired in popular conferences and seminars, only to realize that within weeks of each new self-help effort that you still do not have a statement of personal purpose or any unique, results-producing plan of your very own.

Philosophy, motivation, stimulating conversation and hype around living and working on purpose are just not enough. Eventually, you have to be helped with specifically how to get dynamic results for YOUR life, YOUR family, and YOUR business.

Perhaps you have heard the saying, "If you fail to plan, you plan to fail." Well, for the most part, people do think and perhaps even talk a lot about how they want their lives to be. Unfortunately we just have not been expected or taught how to sufficiently plan to win big at doing what we love. Consequently, we talk ourselves out of pursuing our passions and instead we select the safer options; the more socially acceptable choices at which we are least likely to fail instead.

The opportunity to create and live the life you dream of and deserve is real, *if* and only if you have a strategic, customized, written *life blueprint* and a results-producing *plan of action.*

You at least need a personal mission statement for your life.

The challenge is that most people who are eagerly dreaming and talking about creating stellar lives for themselves, their families, their employees, and their communities don't have any of the above.

They don't have:

- **A strategic, customized, *written life blueprint***
- **A results-producing *plan of action* or;**
- **A personal mission statement for their lives;**

The truth of the matter is that we didn't either.

In 2001, when we created The Destiny Statement™, we did not have a written ***life blueprint*** and a results-producing ***plan of action,*** or ***personal mission statements*** for our lives either. All we had was a deep understanding and respect for why we needed to live purposeful lives.

As professional speakers, we were paid to teach the principles nationally and abroad but when the inspired, excited, encouraged, and often times tearful students and professionals to whom we presented would run up to us after the conferences and seminars, share their stories and testimonies of how the principles and concepts we shared impacted them and would then ask us, "What's next?" We failed to have a satisfactory response to their very logical plea.

With the goal of saving our audiences a lot of money and time by creating a simple, effective process they could employ to discover or clarify their life's work and to apply what we were teaching them, we took our combined 20+ years of skill and expertise as educators and speakers and we synthesized the secrets of the countless masters from whom we have learned.

Even then, we had invested thousands of dollars and hours studying and applying the principles of our teachers who range from experts on purposeful living, getting more done faster, gaining clarity, harnessing the power of vision and so much more. And it was all worth it because from that rich base we created our Destiny Statement™ Process and for more than 15 years and counting it has served as a consistent and effective answer to our audience's plea of, "*What's next?*"

Corporate executives, leaders in various industries, students, parents, pastors, entrepreneurs, authors, coaches, and many others who struggled at some point with what to do with their lives or with what to do next have already experienced documented, sustainable results by learning and implementing the tips and strategies found in *Don't Be Scared. Live on Purpose!* One of our partners called his Destiny Statement™, "*The blueprint for my life.*"

First, we want you to know that we've used the process ourselves. We studied our content and wrote Destiny Statements™ of our own. Then we started to teach and implement the process with family, then friends, then with our students.

Over time, the universities, places of worship, and other organizations who were inviting us in as speakers started to ask us to return to teach the concepts to their people in more detail and to help them get Destiny Statements™ of their own!

Soon, we were not just professional speakers, we were called upon to consult and to coach a diversity of clients. By following the Destiny Statement™ process that we had created, we experienced immediate, long-term, exponential growth in our business and in our lives!

Let's just look at another example of how applying the principles and process shared in the book impacted our lives.

Using the principles we teach, we revised and re-launched as Destiny Statement™ Executive Coaching Programs. Years ago, we started out coaching for as low as $100 per session. We spoke for as low as nothing and for as much as $10,000, but we had very little product to sell. We were very much in our comfort zone. We loved our work. We were successful. But we were not working hard enough at making the BIG plans we had written happen.

After revisiting our written personal missions, visions, etc. we recognized the need to change and to be honest with you; it was quite scary to change what we had been doing with some success for so long. However, in the interest of fulfilling our mission on the level we had said we wanted to, we went to work to make the plans we had written. We threw excuses out of the window and we got to work.

As the founder and CEO of a successful Charter School, authors, speakers, coaches, leaders at our church, team dad to football, mommy taxi, and a host of other things to our family and community we had a lot of very good excuses for staying comfortable in our comfort zone.

Thankfully, we decided to live into our full potential… so we changed.

What do you think happened?

Because we refused to fear following our written plan so that we could make a greater impact in the lives of people with our coaching programs and so that we could play a bigger game overall with our suite of executive coaching services we:

- **Increased the number of people we reached with our coaching programs alone by 164% between 2013 and 2015.**

- **Expanded our coaching packages from as low as $697 per package in 2013 to an average package investment of $5700 in 2015.**

- **By adding a ton of value, following our Destiny Statement™, and refusing to be afraid to change, we grew our coaching income from 4 figures *a year* to *5 figures in 4 months!***

- **Our contracts and sales on coaching alone in the first 4 months of 2015 out produced the entire year of income generated from coaching in 2014 by *$8,330!***

What are people who have benefited from the process shared in *Don't Be Scared. Live on Purpose!* saying?

We shared a success story from our work on the business section of our Destiny Statement™ but we also could have also shared success stories that resulted from our vision statements for our Health and Wellness, Family, Spirit and Character, or from any one of the seven key areas of our statement. Listen to what several of our partners had to say about their experiences with our process:

"The mission statement that Mr. Barlow took me through in high school helped me to realize my dream, put it on paper, and make it happen. It was the first time I truly had to think of my future and what I wanted to do with my life. Looking back, people ask me how I got to where I am today and I reply. . .'Well it started in 9th grade when I wrote a Destiny Statement about what I wanted to study in college and where.' I would not be where I am today, living in Hawaii and pursuing my dreams, without the influence of Mr. Barlow and the writing of my personal mission and vision statements."

Sarah Giannascoli
Zoologist
Honolulu, HI

"The mission statement, the 4 Pillars of Purpose, and the entire Destiny Statement™ and Executive Coaching process definitely helped me. It gave me a foundation of where I need to be, the direction I need to go in, and who I need to be. Dreams are pointless without action. The mission and vision statements helped me write down and put into action what I have dreaming and thinking about. It was a great process!

ShàLaina Sample
Speech Therapist
Philadelphia, PA

"I found writing my mission statement awesome because it instantly boosted my confidence and elevated my clarity regarding my purpose in life and my special talents that I possess. It was life changing, mind altering, and spirit filling."

Dr. André Watson
Psychoanalyst/Psychotherapist
Philadelphia, PA

"Writing my mission statement and reviewing *The Four Pillars of Purpose* allows me to focus and commit to my goals."

Maxine Johnson
Human Resource Executive
Philadelphia, PA

"At eighteen years old attending Jéneen and Omar Barlow's Destiny Statement Conference was crucial in my life. My mission is to encourage, give, and lead; while expressing the values of happiness, kindness, and originality for youth, the homeless, and women's issues. When I wrote that mission statement essentially I was speaking vision and purpose over my life at a young age. This was invaluable. I am currently living out every part of my mission statement to this day. It brings me such a wonderful sense of purpose and identity in this world. I am forever grateful to the Barlows for the gift of helping me discover my hidden potential and purpose through creating a mission statement for my life."

Nicole Giuliani
Elementary School Teacher
Lansdale, PA

The sensational fact is that these phenomenal, consistent results are *not* just reserved for the many, satisfied "Destiny Seekers" we have served to date. You can experience these same real, positive results in your life.

Why not you?

We promise that if you follow the process that we have designed as Phase I of our Destiny Statement™ process that you will be 100% clearer about the reason you exist and we promise that your written personal mission statement will be as unique to you as your fingerprint.

Without a doubt, you will have the most important and most frequently overlooked piece of information that you need in order to take specific, results-producing action. We have literally witnessed the cloud of uncertainty disappear that hovered over so many "successful" people we have helped and be replaced with excited energy for a bright and productive future.

Here's the thing. The only difference between you and the amazing people who we have had the pleasure of helping to find extreme clarity and significance doing their life's work over the years is that

THEY TOOK IMMEDIATE ACTION.

Now, you should too.

Reject the path of the masses that pause, wait, and over-think golden opportunities when these life-changing chances are placed right in their lap. You already sense that if you do not read *Don't Be Scared. Live on Purpose!* you are going to miss out on something life-transforming. So decide not to be the person who misses out when an opportunity is right in front of them. Instead be the person who takes action immediately.

By reading this book you are about to gain access to the specific, proven secrets and strategies that have helped so many others to get immediate, long-term, results-producing change in their lives and businesses. Reject the flawed notion that you cannot discover or clarify your life's work and make an extraordinary living doing what you love.

All you have to do is read it.

We have personally and passionately taught the inspiring insights from each and every single chapter of *Don't Be Scared. Live on Purpose!* with great success for years. As a result, we have seen people gain clarity, celebrate inward revivals, transform deeply, become stunningly more productive, gain new excitement and hope, and create the lives they have dreamed of and deserve.

Join the ranks of this elite, empowered movement of Destiny Seekers now.

We are Master Teachers, Inspirers, and Leaders whose mission is to empower, educate, and equip you to live your full potential. We are as much about your feeling like you can conquer your world as we are about helping you to actually do it! We worked long and hard to perfect a process that would serve as the fail-proof answer to

"What's next?" and we succeeded. Now you get to enjoy the countless benefits of our success.

We're with you all the way so let's get started! Let your Destiny Statement™ process begin . . .

All I know that this is not the job for me. I know that I deserve to earn a lot more money than this company will ever pay me. I know that this is not the college major I should have chosen. I know that I should have broken off this relationship a long time ago. I know that there is more to life than feedings and pampers; laundry and soccer. I know that I should discover or clarify my passion and work at it full-time.

I know that I am here for a reason.

I know. I know. I know! But what is the reason? How do I discover my reason for living? How do I get organized enough to make it happen? How can I summon the boldness I need to crush my fear of doing what I truly love?

The Destiny Statement: Transforming Work, Love and Life

Barlow Enterprises (BE) established the Global Destiny Institute to answer these important questions.

For well over a decade, we have worked with executives, entrepreneurs, speakers, coaches, educators, couples, and students of various ages and socioeconomic statuses. Often our clients are highly educated, unfulfilled executives who are very well-off; some are new or seasoned entrepreneurs; many are collegiate and nonprofit leaders who are looking for outstanding, relevant programming for students or community residents. We also have our beloved high school administrators who need professional and personal development for the students and staff they lead. We have walked beside parents desperate to help their children gain clarity, as well as with couples committed to rediscovering one another.

Regardless of their status in society, every single one of these amazing people with whom we have connected have at least two things in common.

First, they are uncommonly creative, good people. They all have unlimited potential. And each one of them has enriched our lives. Second, they are all people or organizations who sensed that there was some "*thing*" coaxing them beyond where they currently are into a More Excellent domain.

That *thing* is PURPOSE.

We call those who are sensitive to the voice from within, Destiny Seekers. Destiny Seekers are often very clear that there is more available to them but they are also frustrated because sometimes, in their quest for clarity, the *how of living on purpose* eludes them.

How do you begin to answer the call?

You want to work, love, and live on purpose but there are no directions that you can enter into your GPS to get you there and to answer the call to live a life of purpose; and let's face it, we all need directions.

Clear Directions to Your Destiny

Don't Be Scared. Live on Purpose! delivers to you a step-by-step, personalized process that maps the journey from where you are to where you want to be. It helps you to write your Destiny Statement™-- your blueprint for significance and success.

There are numerous best-selling books that discuss why and even how to live a life of purpose. We have read, and we often recommend, many of these texts to others. But while most of these books are filled with inspiring, helpful information, at the end of the read, you are still left without a *personalized* plan that helps you discover and live *your* life on purpose. You are still left saying, "Okay, but how do I figure out *my* mission? What is *my* purpose? How do *I* begin to fulfill it?

For more than a decade, The Destiny Statement™ Institute has helped thousands of individuals write Destiny Statements. In doing so, we have perfected the process and we know how to help you get results.

The Destiny Statement™: Your Ph.D. in Life - YOUR Life!

Clearly, success in life is not solely measured by the accumulation of money, status, and possessions. If it were, then all of those who have sought and attained these things would live free of frustration, depression, and boredom. They would all be happy. Yet we know for certain that wealth and happiness are not synonymous.

As we travel, we often ask our audiences and our clients, "What factors led you to choose your current profession?" "On what basis did you select your mate?" "Why did you decide upon that college major?"

The responses consistently indicate that people make critical life decisions with neither thorough reflection, nor serious consideration about what they would have loved to do or about how making that decision at that time in their life or with that person would alter their future forever.

Sadly, brilliant and gifted people are constantly encouraged and convinced into spending years of their lives studying, testing for, and paying to become credentialed in professions for which they have no true passion.

Consequently, people stumble into lifestyles. For example, because they feared to question and challenge the status quo as it relates to gender or class expectations, many of the people we meet are working when they really want to be staying at home with their children or are staying at home when they would really love to be working. Some hesitate to pursue their dreams because the dream lies in a profession that is traditionally dominated by persons of a certain class, gender, or race that is different from their own. Many are entrepreneurs who are afraid to take action in ways that will explode their incomes and their influence. Put plainly, they live in fear. Nonetheless, living, loving, working on purpose, and being more excellent is about living your life without limits.

School is the place where we all become acculturated. Sadly, our educational institutions rarely, if ever, provide us with any personal development at all. We write hundreds of papers and proposals and graduate with degree upon degree, yet still, we have no solid sense of who we are. No person or institution demands of us a personal mission and vision statement or requires that we know and understand our gifts, talents, and intelligences. None refuse us positions that are not married to our passions and purposes in life. In fact, more often than not, schooling strips us of the innate fearlessness and the love for learning that we possessed as bright-eyed, imaginative children. Sometimes it seems that the more schooling we get, the more afraid we become.

Writing your Destiny Statement™ is the most important use of your time and energy that you will ever invest as it relates to your personal development. Essentially, **The Destiny Statement™** is the Dissertation or Thesis Statement of your life.

It is the anchor or compass that no institution of higher education requires, yet without this guide, your work, love, and life overall are incessantly found yearning for more.

The Destiny Statement: Inspires and Equips You Live Your More Excellent Life

Instead of rigorous self-study, discovery, and interest-based action, people advise, "Live your dreams later; after your degrees and money are earned. Just do well in school, get a good job with good benefits, work hard, and raise your family first. Fulfill your dreams . . . later."

No! No! No! We are committed to challenging and changing that mindless, heartless, fear-filled notion. Instead, we have come to inspire a generation of people to reject that norm and to instead do as Mark Twain said, "Don't let your schooling interfere with your education." As parents, educators, and lifelong learners ourselves, we highly value education; it is the *system of schooling* that we seek to reform. We come to swoop down into the lives of the many brilliant and talented children, women, and men who are beginning to discover, working to clarify, or have forgotten their dreams, with a message of inspiration and a with a practical process that quickly begins to move them from ordinary to extraordinary. **The Destiny Statement™** is the solution.

The Destiny Statement: Transforming School Systems For The 21st Century

The Destiny Statement™ transforms traditional school systems' modes of education and provides an instrument for learners an administrators that support their efforts to educate learners one person at a time.

We see the powerful impact of having students in grades K through sixteen develop mission and vision statements which describe how they see themselves in the seven key areas of life.

Our most successful efforts with clients and students have as the culminating work, a customized portfolio that includes mission and vision statements; gifts, talents and intelligences; yearly, monthly, and daily goals and action plans; dream lists; bibliographies tailored to their areas of interests for each of the seven key areas of life; and three, five, ten, fifteen, and twenty year life-plans.

The Destiny Statement Process™, serves to inform people's academic and social lives. It helps clients avoid making critical mistakes and provides them with essential information with which to make important life decisions. We have witnessed how much clarity students, couples, entrepreneurs, and other professionals gain when they commit to the process. They become more focused, more confident, and much, much more productive. In fact, our clients often share that after using the process they produce more results, with more satisfaction, much more quickly, and on a consistent basis.

The Destiny Statement: Authors' Experience Evidence Everyday -- It Works!

We are married business partners and the parents of three young children who serve or have served as educators and executive administrators at both the high school and university levels for more than two decades combined. We are also successful entrepreneurs. So, based on our experiences and on our research, we have unique perspectives about the enormous short and long-term impacts of addressing the personal purpose deficit.

I (Omar) currently serve as the Founding CEO and Principal of Eastern University Academy Charter School (EUACS), the first Passion-Based, Early College inspired High School in Philadelphia, PA. Prior to leading EUACS, I taught at the second largest suburban high school in the state for 8 years.

As a high school teacher I was most frustrated that after scores of quizzes, tests, papers and projects, students consistently proved to be unaware of what they wanted to do with their lives. So, while I had to teach my students English, I chose to also teach them about life. I became well-known and loved by my students. They nicknamed me *"**The Life Teacher**."* Because of my mission in life, I reveal to learners the *Hidden Curriculum of Life*. This is the curriculum that is vital, but so often ignored.

Consider again, the words of Mark Twain: "Do not let your schooling interfere with your education."

It is easier for learners to disregard attempts at real discovery and pursuit of purpose in exchange for careers that are socially acceptable or careers that will earn them a lot of money (and there is nothing wrong with earning a lot of money). However, living a life of purpose requires that we move beyond mere schooling and enter into the beautifully demanding, yet exceptionally rewarding, world of education.

For most of us, attaining more schooling, by going to college or learning a trade without going through a process that enables us to become clear about our mission, vision, gifts, and goals, only makes life more confusing.

I recall a former student who came back to me and said, "Mr. Barlow, I have absolutely no idea what I would like to do. Maybe I will try marketing. That's what everyone in my family is doing. But, honestly, it just seems that I am just wasting $30,000 a year."

When students have this story, it is clear that irrespective of how well a school scores in their math and reading standardized exams, that they fail in an important aspect of preparing students to succeed. Why else, after at least twelve years of "schooling," do so many students remain clueless about what they would really love to do with their lives and about how to make that happen for themselves?

As we travel, as well as, in my own schools, I have conducted thousands of surveys of students helping them to identify their gifts, talents, and dominant intelligences. Initially, most of the students are clueless. This is a problem. I am not even asking students to have all of their lives figured out, but the problem lies in the fact that schools do not require us to develop our potential at all.

The Destiny Statement: A Lifejacket for Drifting Dreamers

Let's consider graduation. Things really can become complicated when one graduates and is forced to survive the onslaught of the responsibilities that marriage, children, and bills demand. Things become more desperate. Life can become overwhelming. Often it is at graduation, after being asked what our next steps will be, that the wise among us declare with false confidence, "*Oh, well, I . . . I am going to graduate school.*" This, for many can be translated,

"I've been told that I won't earn enough money doing what I'd really love to do. Besides, the fact that going to graduate school is a socially acceptable reply, I sincerely do not know what I want to do with this meaningless degree or with my life in general. Indeed, I am petrified of being thrust into the real world just yet."

Inevitably, most people eventually yield to the norm of getting a job. For many, this is time during which people come face to face with the revelation that they are on a road to who knows where. It is understandable how it happens, but something must be done. So, as a team committed to providing an adequate response to two of life's most pressing dilemmas -- purposelessness and lack of planning and taking action in ways that yield desired results -- we created **The Destiny Statement™**.

We have been teaching our processes across the nation for over a decade. Now, we present these seminars to you in this book.

We know that it works. We have worked with thousands of people. We have designed programs, written curriculum for, and piloted programs of our own, as well as for non-profit organizations, public and private elementary and secondary schools, and universities. We have taught to groups and mentored individuals through the process in various ways over the years. We've discarded the things that do not work and carefully added depth and value along the way. Most of all, we consistently apply our learning and teaching to our own lives and to our children's lives.

We live what we teach.

And we are compelled to share it because in spite of the fact that it is not easy to apply the principles of living a disciplined and purposeful life, it works!

We take your life and your time seriously so we want you to know what to expect from this book.

What you read will be both inspirational and practical.

You will become increasingly aware of the significance of your life and how small changes in your thinking can totally revolutionize your life. You will discover and begin to understand and appreciate yourself and what you have to offer in new ways. You will begin to develop a personalized document that enables you to spend the majority of your time joyfully living out your purpose and destiny.

In the words of Confucius,

> *Give a man a fish and he will eat for a day, teach a man how to fish and he will eat for a lifetime.*

It is in the spirit of this proverb, that we offer you a lifejacket in the form of these lessons on how to Work. Love. Live and Be More Excellent.

Get your pen and go to work, Destiny Seeker. These lessons have enriched our lives and our legacy. We will certainly never be the same.

May you experience blessings so full that your life and your legacy are positively impacted forever!

Chapter Introductions

Chapter one, *The Four Pillars of Purpose: A Philosophy of Purpose,* explains why it is essential to live a life of purpose by defining purpose and by discussing the fundamental philosophy of purposeful living. We introduce you to the Four Pillars of Purpose. These four principles, when understood and engaged, transform your thinking and catapult you into living a life of fulfillment and clarity.

In ***Just Ask***, chapter two, we introduce you to the powerful principle of asking questions. Your life is ultimately made of the questions that you ask and the questions that you refuse to ask. Unfortunately, we learn as children to become afraid of asking penetrating, thought provoking questions. We defy that norm by equipping you with the information you need to ask the right types of questions.

Part II of the book, The Destiny Statement™ Fundamental Five, is equivalent to ballet classes of the dance world, classical music classes of the music world, and to life drawing classes in the world of visual arts because in chapters three through seven you learn the fundamentals to purposeful living. One of the hallmarks of a purposeful living is discipline. A life lived on purpose is a disciplined life. In these chapters, we arm you with the five essential questions that you must ask and answer in order to live a purposeful life. If you seriously consider and write the answers to these questions, you will transform your life.

The first of The Destiny Statement™ Fundamental Five is the Identity Question. Primarily through a discussion of the extremely transformational power of your words, Chapter 3 explores the purpose question: *Who am I?*

After you answer the Who am I? question, Chapter 4 walks you even closer to discovering or refining your purpose by answering the Source Question: *Where do I come from?* In this chapter, you will analyze the various components of source and explain why it is absolutely critical to become very clear about how you identify your source.

Chapter 5 is the heartbeat of the entire text. Here we carefully walk through some of the major questions that Destiny Seekers have to think about, write answers to, and take action upon. In this chapter, we explore the Purpose Question:

Why am I here? as well as, seven of the most Popular purpose sub-questions.

Once you consider and write your answers to the questions of purpose, you will begin to understand what freedom and fun comes with answering: *What can I do*? This is **The Gifts Question** and in Chapter 6 we discuss how to use the gifts that come naturally to you to create a life that you will love.

In Chapter 7 we explore **The Vision Question**. Here the excitement truly sets in because all that you have thought about and written as we walked through **Don't Be Scared! Live on Purpose** takes shape as we review the role of vision in living on purpose and learn from the three famous case studies: Oprah Winfrey, Stephen Spielberg, and J.K. Rowlings. These stellar individuals fearlessly pursued their visions and their decision to do so led to extraordinary success for all of them. Question number five is *Where am I going?*

We teach in various venues and without fail our audiences say, "Okay, you have explained The Destiny Statement™ Philosophy of Purpose and given me these five essential questions on which to reflect and write, now what?" Chapter 8,

Living on Mission, shows you exactly how to write your personal mission statement.

In Chapter 8 we explain exactly what the The Destiny Statement™ contains and why we think it is criminal for anyone to graduate with a degree, diploma, or certificate of any kind without a Destiny Statement™. We walk you through the very first step in the process of writing your Destiny Statement™. Writing your Destiny Statement™ begins with writing your personal mission statement. Knowing the philosophy of living a purposeful life is not enough. You need a written down reason for being of your very own. We have helped thousands of people nationally and internationally to write custom mission statements for their lives and in three concise and effective steps and we can't wait to show you exactly how to craft a customized personal mission statement of your own.

Writing your mission statement is like placing your fingerprint in eternity. You will not leave chapter eight without a written down reason of your very own!

After you have written your custom mission statement, you will be ready to move on to the next several phases of writing your Destiny Statement™ as explained in:

Don't Be Scared. Live on Purpose! Volume II

- Writing Your Vision in the Seven Key Areas of Life

Don't Be Scared. Live on Purpose! Volume III

- Identifying Your Intelligences
- Identifying Your Strengths and Gifts
- Choosing Your Destiny-Driven Deadlines

CHAPTER 1

The 4 Pillars of Purpose

Within the soul of every human being there is a hunger for one's purpose. Everyone wants to know, "Why am I here?" What is my contribution to life? The purpose of life is not to be happy, it is to be useful, honorable, to be compassionate, and to have it make some difference that you have lived and lived well.
~ Richard Leider

This is the true joy in life, being used for a purpose you consider a mighty one, being a force of nature rather than a feverish, selfish clod of ailments and grievances complaining that the world will not devote itself to making you happy.
~ George B. Shaw

The greatest tragedy in life is not death, but it is life without a reason.
~ Dr. Myles Munroe

Purpose can be defined as the original intent for the creation of a thing. Purpose is the reason for which you exist.

Purpose declares that because you were born into a world of over 6 billion people, and not one has your fingerprint, that you were created for a reason. You may not feel like you have everything that you need to move forward. Yet, purpose insists that, in spite of your flaws, you accept your responsibility to use what you have to discover, pursue and become who you desire to be. You are responsible to do what you were destined to do so that you reach who you were destined to reach. As a Destiny Seeker you live with the weight, and the joy, of the fact that someone is waiting for you to do something that only you can do so that they can fulfill their dreams too.

Living on purpose is about living in the big questions of life. It is a life-altering perspective which supersedes materialism, status, and fame.

People may use all of these things to enjoy life, nonetheless fantastic things will never satisfy the soul that truly longs to live a meaningful life. We have met and read of many whom have all of the material things one can acquire, yet many of them still feel empty and unfulfilled. On the surface, acquiring things seems so important, but when you live in the big questions of life, acquiring things alone pales in comparison to what you gain when you make the time to answer the fundamental questions of life and then work to realize your vision.

At its core, living on purpose is about living with reasons, for while there is tragedy in death, death is not the greatest tragedy. On the contrary, the greatest tragedy is living your life without a crystal clear reason.

Until you discover your purpose, your existence has no meaning. Let us introduce you to The Global Destiny Institute's Four Pillars of Purpose.

Pillar #1: Check Your Heart

> *He hath made everything beautiful in his time: also he hath set the world (eternity) in their heart, so that no man can find out the work that God maketh from the beginning to end.*
>
> ~ *Ecclesiastes 3:11*

What lies behind us and what lies before us are tiny matters compared to what lies within us.

~ Ralph Waldo Emerson

Keys symbolize authority and access. The following proverb is the guiding force of the Destiny Statement™ process and it is the key to understanding and applying pillar one in your life.

Purpose in the heart of a man is like deep water; but a man of understanding will draw it out.

~Proverbs 20:5

Your purpose is surprisingly close to you.

The author says that your purpose is in your heart. Purpose is placed in your heart so that you can find it! It is not far from you but you must make the time to quiet yourself, listen for your heart's voice, and take careful note of what the voice is telling you. Your purpose resides in your subconscious mind or in your heart, but it is only by asking the right questions that you can become aware of exactly what lives there.

Your subconscious mind is your figurative heart. It is fascinating that in your heart rests passions, desires, intents, causes, ideas, themes, and dreams; things that you feel drawn to; and things that you feel compelled to do. When you are not conscious, you may not know why you are drawn to certain causes, ideas, themes, and dreams. But the drawing has everything to do with your heart's cry for you stop and listen to her instructing you on how to fulfill your life's purpose.

Unfortunately, most people do not access what is in their heart because they do not stop. They do not listen. Instead, they live unconsciously preoccupied with so many nebulous things that eventually they are quietly, subtly pulled away from all that really matters.

A proverb says,

> *Guard your heart with all diligence, for out it flow the issues of life.*

In other words, there are secrets and solutions right in your heart, and it is your responsibility to guard, or to protect and take care of it.

Observe almost any child, and you will see someone who is in tune with their heart. Children are free spirits. If they feel like singing, they sing. If they feel like dancing, they dance. And if they say that they are a movie star or a scientist that is who they are, for that moment in time, because they believe it.

Children, before we socialize the life and honesty out of them, often freely express the purity of their thoughts and beliefs. They have not learned to live in fear. Children do not live with the reservations that grip us in adulthood. Children do not care what adults think, and that is one of the reasons they are so fascinating (and at times frustrating).

Perhaps this is why the scriptures tell us to, come as a child and why the famous poet William Wordsworth so eloquently reminds us that, *"Our birth is but a sleep and a forgetting."* Just maybe we forget at birth who we were in eternity. Yet children easily tap into that memory. They are closest to their birth, so purpose lingers and speaks clearly to them in childhood. Memories of who they were whisper to them and those memories instruct their play and fuel their freedom.

We encourage our Executive Partners and our audiences to think about and to ask others who knew them as children, how they were, what they enjoyed doing, and what they used to imagine or say they would become. That type of research of self gives you a glimpse into your passion and purpose in life. So many of the answers you long for are right in your heart.

In Randy Pausch's best-selling book, *The Last Lecture,* he discusses the power of his own childhood dreams. In the face of his courageous bout with pancreatic cancer, Pausch wrote the book. Because the cancer was terminal, he wanted to offer the world critical, life-lessons before his death. It is telling that he reminds his readers to pay close attention to the lessons we can learn from the innocence of childhood dreams. As you embark upon living, loving, and working on purpose it is essential that you *Check Your Heart.*

Pillar #2: ***Dive Deep***

> *Purpose in the heart of a man is like deep water, but a man of understanding will draw it out.*
>
> ~ *Proverbs 20:5*

Pillar two of The Global Destiny Institute's philosophy of purpose is Dive Deep. The proverb claims that your purpose is like deep water. Think about what water represents. It is a life-sustaining source. Water represents renewal and is refreshing. This is what your purpose is like inside of you. So when you discover and then begin to live out your purpose, you will actually begin to enliven, renew, and refresh every person and everything in your sphere of influence.

People will live better lives when *you* live on purpose.

While you are wasting precious seconds questioning whether you are good enough, someone is dying. They are dying to read your book. Someone is longing to hear your music. Someone is being overlooked because you are not his teacher. Someone is waiting for you to invent something.

Face it, when you dare to live on purpose you position yourself to refresh someone's world. When you are working, loving, and living on purpose you will revitalize someone's life!

In considering the proverb we need to consider why purpose is likened not just to water, but to *deep* water.

Why deep water?

Deep ocean water, also known as DOW, is located in the Earth's oceans. This very cold water is found deep below the surface of the ocean and it is salty. On the contrary, water found at the surface of the ocean is warm and is relatively non-salty. Most interestingly, when deep water is brought to the surface, its uses, primarily due to the temperature of the water, multiply. Scientists say that the difference in temperature indicates a difference in energy. If that energy gradient is handled by skillful professionals, the energy can be put to productive use for humankind.

We could not create a more perfect analogy. Purpose is like deep water. Just as deep ocean water is buried beneath the earth's surface, your purpose and vision lie in wait deep within your heart.

Your life's purpose is like salt and ice. It is salty and cold because it has the ability to preserve and to revive you, and those to whom you are sent. No matter your wealth, success, or misfortune if you work on bringing your purpose out of the depth and to the surface, the limitless uses of your life will immediately multiply.

Destiny Seekers, you will work, love, live and become more excellent when you:

- Check Your Heart
- Dive Deep

Pillar #3: Seek Understanding

> *Purpose in the heart of man is like deep water, but a man of understanding will draw it out.*
>
> *~Proverbs 20:5*

After you have checked your heart and braved the deep, work to identify, understand, and engage people of understanding.

We marvel at the number of people who are thankful for the work that we have done. After speaking many say, thank you so much for giving me a sense of purpose. We appreciate their gratitude, but we have to constantly remind them that we did not *give* them anything. We just helped them to "draw out" what was *already* inside of them. This is exactly what the proverb means. When you understand yourself, you can pull out the treasures within, and when you don't, it will take meeting someone – women and men of understanding – who draw your purpose out of you.

In as much as meeting the right person can unlock your potential, encounters and relationships with the wrong people can stunt your development.

Many already know your potential. They can sense your greatness. Some are enemies of your purpose and others are friends. Regardless, sometimes people refuse to give you the information or the affirmation that you need in order for you to excel. And sometimes, the person who is most afraid for you to succeed is you.

Victor Frankl, Jewish Holocaust survivor and author of *Man's Search for Meaning*, claims,

"We detect rather than invent our personal [purpose] in life."

When deep water is brought from the Earth's oceans, the energy it has changes. Similarly, once your purpose is brought out of obscurity, you will possess an uncommon energy. And, when your purpose is drawn out by people of understanding; skillful coaches, mentors, and carriers of purpose themselves, your purpose will be put to special and productive use for all of the people who are literally *waiting* for you to enrich the earth with your gifts, talents, passions, and dreams.

Destiny Seekers, you will work, love, live and become more excellent when you:

- Check Your Heart
- Dive Deep
- Become a Person of Understanding & Seek Out People of Understanding

Pillar #4: Flow

Last of all, with all that you find out you have to find out how to flow!

Metaphysics is the study of how the invisible realm informs the physical; how the unseen informs the seen. Ancient scholars suggest that the creator placed eternity in our hearts before we were born. In essence, before you were born, the creator placed something eternal (outside of time) in your heart.

Consequently, when you discover your life's purpose, you love it so much that in the process of fulfilling it you often lose track of time.

Why? Because eternity transcends time; when you are working on purpose, you are working out the eternity that was set in your heart -- before you were born. Therefore, you transcend the physical limitations of time and step, again, into an eternal or timeless realm.

The extraordinary life of Vincent Van Gogh gives us a glimpse of how embracing and working on your passion enables you to transcend the barriers of time.

Van Gogh struggled terribly to find his purpose and passion in life. In fact, he was a teacher, a preacher, and a clerk in an art gallery before he ever began to paint the magnificent masterpieces the world beholds today. He struggled to find his purpose. Even more interestingly, he did not begin to paint until he was twenty-seven years of age. Yet because he had finally discovered his purpose, time was not an issue. It is said that Van Gogh rendered over 800 paintings and countless other drawings over the next ten years of his life. He could often be found feverously painting around the clock forgoing and forgetting both sleep and meals.

Clearly, when he was painting, he was out of time and although he ended his life tragically, the fact that he lived, loved, and worked passionately, is what made his life worth living. Remember, living on purpose is about living with reasons. For while there is tragedy in death, it is living a life without purpose, not dying, that is the greatest tragedy of all.

Athletes and musicians also understand what it means to transcend time in the process of working toward a goal. They call it "the zone" or "the groove." When you enter the zone, you step into a zany realm and you feel that you cannot be stopped once you enter there. When you are in your zone, enemies and friends alike, recognize that you are different. When you start to groove, your focus and positive energy literally propel you into another realm of happiness. Time stands still. When you commit to the process of discovering or refining your purpose and living it out, you make a choice to live in the zone -- to live a life that gifts you with the pure joy and freedom of doing what you want and love to do.

Dr. Mihaly Csíkszentmihályi, the brilliant Hungarian philosopher of psychology and author of the seminal work *Flow: The Psychology of Optimal Experience,* theorizes that the state at which we reach complete absorption in an activity is the state at which we achieve flow. While the biographies and autobiographies of artists and musicians lend us the most famous examples of individuals who reach these optimal states of intrinsic motivation or flow, in your quest to live your more excellent life, it is important for you to realize that the flow to which Dr. Csíkszentmihályi refers is not reserved for athletes and artists.

Flow, according to Csíkszentmihályi in an interview with *Wired* magazine, is to become completely involved in an activity for its own sake. The ego falls away. Time flies. Every action, movement, and thought follows inevitably from the previous one, like playing jazz. Designers, hikers, physicians, students, childcare workers, teachers, gardeners, counselors, administrators, and activists alike can experience flow. Indeed, as long as you are totally and completely absorbed with the activity at hand, no matter what the activity is, you can flow too.

The Four Pillars Summarized

Check your heart. Listen for what your subconscious is trying to tell you. Dive deep. You will become supernaturally energized. Understand that you must connect with the right people. And you will trade boredom and anxiety for a life of working and playing in flow. The key to unlocking your purpose is right inside of you merely awaiting your recognition of it!

These are the four pillars on which living more excellently stand. Choose to give this process the time and energy necessary and you will attain the states of happiness, contentment, and synergy that you need to live YOUR more excellent life. To download a free Mp3 training of the *Four Pillars of Purpose* now visit

www.destinystatement.com.

Destiny Seekers, you will work, love, live and become more excellent when you:

- Check Your Heart
- Dive Deep
- Become a Person of Understanding & Seek Out People of Understanding
- Flow

The Destiny Seekers' Challenge:

The Four Pillars of Purpose are established as guideposts for purposeful living. The pillars offer you a foundation from which to begin to discover, refine, and live a meaningful life. Since living a more excellent life requires extraordinary energy, the proverb helps to focus and ground you. It is the place to which you can always return to assess your progress, to plan, and to be renewed on your quest to live more excellent lives.

Memorize the Four Pillars of Purpose.

Tweet your favorite Pillar to @BeMorExcellent or post it on Barlow Enterprises Facebook page now. Tell us why that pillar most impacted you.

We'll follow you back!

CHAPTER 2

Just Ask

Life begins with questions. Nothing shapes our lives as much as the questions we ask, or refuse to ask.

~ Richard Leider

[illegible]

Asking is the beginning of receiving.

Jesus said, *"Ask and it shall be given to you."* Could it be that simple? Are you not living your more excellent life because you have failed to ask your way into it?

There are numerous things that you need to be able to do in order for you to live an excellent life. One of them is to ask excellent questions. In order to activate the life transforming power of the four pillars of purpose discussed in chapter one, you have to master the skill of asking questions.

In this chapter, we introduce you to the primary types of questions that you can ask yourself and others. Unless you learn to grapple with and answer questions, you will not be able to discover, articulate, or refine your life's purpose.

Don't think. Don't care. Just ASK.

Our children and our work with young people are daily reminders to us of the power of asking questions.

I (Omar) will never forget taking my son, Joshua, and my nephew, Isaiah, to a local diner. We frequented the diner, so the boys knew the lay of the land. Before we could even park, they began to ask me for quarters because they wanted gum and toys from the machines in the lobby area. My silence held them off until we entered the building, but once we were inside I told them that I did not have any quarters. Without pause, these two fearless, focused boys, only 4 and 7 at the time, proceeded to ask the adults around us for quarters.

Of course I stopped them from disturbing the patrons and reminded them of the potentially unsafe practice of taking money, or anything, from strangers. I was embarrassed by their behavior, but I learned an important lesson. The boys were practicing the principle of asking.

After we had eaten our meal, the boys remembered that they did not have quarters and quickly forgot my correction. As I was paying they said to the cashier, "Excuse me, do you have quarters?" They figured that if anyone had quarters she would! Joshua and Isaiah were still focused on their goal -- to get something out of those machines. They did not care what people would say. As a matter of fact, they did not even think about what people would say. They knew what they wanted. I did not have it. So, they began to ask others. They would not stop questioning.

If we are to be taken seriously, we must abide by certain societal norms, but the moral of the boys' story is that we often fail to do the simple things that we can do or say in order to get what we need because we are paralyzed, and therefore silenced, by the fear of what others will think, do, or say.

Our internal motivations for want we want must be so strong that they provoke us to do things that will in some cases defy the status quo, and in most cases, push us from our comfort zones. Kids live without those inhibitions. The great scientist Albert Einstein said,

> *The important thing is to not stop questioning. Curiosity has its own reason for existing. One cannot help but be in awe when he contemplates the mysteries of eternity, of life, of the marvelous structure of reality. It is enough if one tries merely to comprehend a little of this mystery each day. Never lose a holy curiosity.*

Learn from Joshua and Isaiah's example. Apply the tenacity of these young boys for a small thing to your big dreams. And when fear of what others will think, say, or do comes to slow or stop your progress, don't think, don't care. Just ask.

Don't be Afraid to Ask Tough Questions

Our pensive son Joshua has always asked very deep questions. He asked questions such as: "Where was I before I was born?" "Who made me?" "Where is heaven?" "How do I get there?" "How do I get back?" "Did Pop-Pop and Mike go to heaven?" "When are they coming back?" "How are they going to get back?"

He's also asks questions about mundane events. For example, after a trip to the bank together

Joshua asked, "Why do you keep your money in that bank? How do you know that someone won't steal it? "What do they do with the money any-way?" He was four.

Our Grace also asks a lot of questions. Perhaps because she is two years younger than Joshua, or just super spunky, she is most apt to ask those "inquiring minds want to know" types of ques-tions – questions we all want to ask but know that we should not.

When Gracie was two she saw a woman with a tattoo in the center of her chest. We were in church. Before we could stop Grace she had asked, "What is that?" The woman kindly replied, "A tattoo." Then my daughter asked, "Why did you get it? By her tone and her facial expressions it was clear that Miss Grace did not approve of the tattoo. The silence was pregnant. It was one of those moments in which you wished you could beam yourself somewhere else.

Beaming myself up was not an option, but thankfully remembering the advice of Lord Bud-dha was. And it helped. It was Buddha who said,

> *There are these four ways of answering questions. Which four? There are questions that should be answered categorically [straightforwardly yes, no, this, or that]. There are questions that should be answered with an analytical (qualified) answer [defining or redefining the terms]. There are questions that should be answered with a counter-question. There are questions that should be put aside. These are the four ways of answering questions.*

While the woman decided how to answer Miss Grace, we politely chose Buddha's door number four, smiled, and excused ourselves. Although we tabled Gracie's question that day, Grace reminds us of an important lesson. Don't be afraid to ask tough questions.

Ask More Excellent Questions. Get More Excellent Results.

While hosts of teachers, counselors and speakers teach about the power of asking questions, few do so as effectively as master motivator and peak performance coach, Mr. Anthony Robbins. Robbins explains that,

> *The main difference between people who seemed successful in any area and those who weren't was*

that successful people asked better questions and as a result, they got better answers.

Robbins argues that you can change your life if you change the questions you habitually ask and if you commit to asking empowering questions in positive, as well as, difficult times."

Asking the empowering, or what we call, the propelling question, is so important because the questions you ask influence the answers you get and the answers that you get either propel, or prohibit, you from thinking, writing, and taking action. It is the quality of your questions that get you closer to or farther away from your destiny. Asking is paramount because what you ask greatly influences what you get.

HALTS Hungry, Angry, Lonely, Tired, Scared!

Before asking and answering purpose questions, our minds and hearts need to prepare for the journey. Consider the following:

- **Are you asking the right questions, of the right people, at the right time?**
- **Are your questions framed in a manner that elicits a response that does not limit your possibilities?**

- **Are you prepared to embrace only answers that will move you from where you are to where you want to be?**
- **Are you prepared to quickly reject answers that lure you into the past or make you feel stuck where you are now?**

HALTS, the acronym often used in addiction and stress management, stands for ***hungry, angry, lonely, tired, and scared***. Because these are major stress triggers which attract negative instead of positive energy which could potentially lead addicts to relapse, those in recovery are taught never to get too lonely, angry, hungry, tired or scared.

While this may be life-saving advice for recovering addicts, this is excellent advice for us all. If you are hungry, angry, lonely, tired or scared you should pay attention to these states of being before you begin asking and answering the questions that follow.

On the other hand, these fragile conditions could be the seedbeds you need to propel you into purpose. For some it is hunger, anger, fatigue, loneliness, fear or some other uncomfortable situation through which the discovery of your purpose occurs. Some people need to fully feel these discomforts before their passions come to light.

So, don't HALT asking questions when faced with these conditions or emotions. But do assess carefully whether you can receive the most excellent answers based upon the emotions, the questions, the time, and the people present at that moment. Should you wait? Do you need to change something about your emotion, tone, or question? Should you ask someone else? Will the emotions, circumstances, or people present cloud the way in which you process the reply? There is no one right answer. Actually, there are infinite answers depending upon the situation.

Our point is that you need to be aware of your physical and emotional states, as well as, the states of others before you ask, answer, and receive the answers to questions that affect your destiny.

Stop, Listen & Get Where You Belong!

No matter how patient you are, if you have ever parented or even cared for children in any capacity for any length of time you have been heard saying something like this (probably at the top of your lungs), "Children! Stop what you are doing immediately. Listen carefully, and get where you belong!"

Now, if it were shouted at them, most adults would cringe at or simply ignore such a command. Nonetheless, stopping all that you are doing immediately and listening to someone more experienced than you, are usually the two major steps that have to happen before you can get where you belong. And living on purpose will not occur unless you *"**get where you belong.**"*

As he'd faithfully ask me critical questions and nudge me on throughout the process of completing this work I'd (Jéneen) often snap at one of my dearest friends, "Don't you think I thought of that, Reem? You're always challenging and correcting. How about this? Just stop telling me what to do!" Thankfully, we've been friends since high school and he knows my ways so he just quietly replies, "Only Omar could put up with you." In spite of my belligerence, there was not one time that I did not stop, listen, and reposition myself because of Karim's, or any other mentor and friends', questions and feedback. Why?

Because pride and resistance will not get you where you belong.

It truly does not matter how successful or how unsuccessful you, or others, think you are. People who are determined to create extraordinary futures for themselves and for others understand that in order to do so they must become consistent, skilled evaluators, and perceptive risk-takers. Pride and resistance to uncertainty have no place among Destiny Seekers. By being careful to allow my mentors and friends' critique and questions to lead me into processes of reflection, evaluation, and action, I always leave the process with more clarity about how to get from where I am at that moment to where I belong.

Consequently, serious Destiny Seekers are humble, flexible, expert evaluators who make informed decisions based upon, listening with care, writing for clarity, and strategically taking action to position themselves exactly where they belong on time or early.

Are you where you belong?

With this in mind, revisit questions three and four above and write your answers. Ask yourself:

- **Have I prepared myself to only embrace answers that which will move me from where I am to where I want to be?**

- **Am I prepared to quickly reject answers that lure me into the past or that make me feel stuck in my current situation?**

Don't resist the process.

It is not assumed that you are not a success if you are considering these questions. Sometimes it is the most successful among us who are the most frustrated. The multitalented individual finds herself in need of constant intellectual stimulation and in need of new challenges as projects are successfully completed and new projects begin. Often, the successful are bombarded with requests from others for their time, as well as, with multiple ideas of their own which they need to organize, delegate, or decide whether to pursue at all. As a result, the challenge of doing many things well can become as daunting as not knowing what to do at all. Sometimes where you are is good. Sometimes it is not. It does not matter which is the case for you. The real question that purpose asks of you is, ***"Do you sense that, regardless of whether you are happy or miserable, you are where you belong?"***

When in pursuit of your passion and purpose, it is often the cozy places of the past and present that are your worst enemies. Some places of our past look and feel good but they are not where we belong.

On the other hand, in an effort to recover or restore situations and relationships in our lives that were life-giving but that we may have abandoned for some reason, sometimes we need to revisit our pasts.

So be careful not to assume that looking back always results in you ending up in a detrimental space. Just know and be honest about which is the case for you.

Acknowledge your truth and move forward.

Vacate Your Comfort Zone

Our innate instinct to relax too long in the comfort zones of life can cause us to fall prey to the trappings of good fortune. Sometimes you are offered opportunities that are excellent but to which you just need to say no because of the season that you are in at that time on your path.

For example, saying yes to a magnificent promotion and pay increase at a time when you should actually be finishing recording your song in the studio, travelling to care for a sick in-law, spending more time building your part-time business or pouring yourself into a child in need, may yield more money and status but will not deliver you joy or peace if you are not where you belong. In essence, you must be in the right place at the right time in order to **Live on Purpose!**

Living a life of passion and purpose constantly challenges you and requires you "daily" to vacate your comfort zone. Now that you have been reminded, go forward, ask more excellent questions, and get more excellent results!

Read the following questions aloud and pay attention to the difference in the way you feel when asking a prohibitive question versus the way you feel when you ask a propelling question.

Prohibitive Questions	**Propelling Questions**
What good is this?	How can I use this?
What is this happening to me?	Because of this, what will I be able to contribute to others?
Why don't I have anything?	What do I still have?
Why can't I ever do anything right?	What can I do?
What can I do now that I am disabled?	Who am I really? What can I do? What do I

	have to offer to others independent of the function that I lost?
Why did I take this risk? Why did I give so much of myself and time to that project or person?	What am I capable of now, even more than before?
Why did I have these children?	What activities can I do with my children to get to know and enjoy them more? What do my children have to contribute to me and to others?
Why don't I have enough time to get anything done?	How can I use the time I have most effectively? How can I better manage my tasks and become more organized?
Why can't I score in the top range on these exams?	How can I better prepare to pass these exams? What adjustments do I need to make to reach my desired score?
Why don't they ever recognize my work?	What can I do to make my work more recognizable?

Why did I do this? Why did I even take this risk?	What is the downside? What's the worst that can happen?
How am I ever going to be able to handle this?	How can I begin to handle this?
Why don't you want to spend time with me?	How can I use this time alone to renew myself?

The Five Fundamental Questions of Life

Now that we have practiced translating prohibitive questions into propelling questions, there are five particular questions that will thrust you into clarity. We call these the fundamental questions of life. The questions are:

1. **Who am I?**
2. **Where did I come from?**
3. **Why am I here?**
4. **What can I do?**
5. **Where am I going?**

Several years ago, while conducting a couples' seminar on the significance of discovering individual and shared purposes, we noticed how disturbed one gentleman appeared. We were in the middle of helping his wife and him complete their

Destiny Statements but he was too frustrated for us to continue. When we inquired why he seemed so flustered he confessed, "*You two just keep asking me things that I don't even want to think about!*" We all laughed and helped him through it, but he is not alone.

We have worked with thousands of individuals from diverse backgrounds. Our partners have included, teachers, parents, families, entrepreneurs, corporate and nonprofit executives, grade school and high school students. Without fail, the evaluations we receive and the stories of those who write us after training with us reveal that people are initially frustrated with, and often resistant to reflecting upon and answering the big questions of life.

Sometimes these questions evoke feelings of regret, fear, or guilt, but people eventually relax into the process and when they do so, their rewards are tremendous.

Regardless of your initial response to this process, it is essential that you give yourself permission and time to answer the questions because your decision to get through the excitement, guilt, anxiety, lack of patience, fear, and other emotions that *will* visit you during a process like this is the decision that will lead you to significant clarity.

You will trade regret for confidence, fear for courage, procrastination for action, and confusion for clarity.

Take the risk!

Before you continue to explore the five fundamental questions of life, take a few minutes to review The Four Pillars of Purpose from chapter one.

- **Check your Heart**
- **Dive Deep**
- **Seek Understanding**
- **Flow**

The Destiny Seeker's Challenge:

What two types of questions did we discuss in this chapter? We talked about:

Propelling questions - Prohibitive questions

Write one to three of the most threatening or prohibitive questions you ask yourself here: ____

Translate the prohibitive questions into propelling questions. Write the revised questions here:

Just by completing the Destiny Seeker Challenges in chapters one and two, you have made excellent progress already!

Share your progress. Tweet what you learned or what inspired you most from this chapter to @BeMorExcellent or post it on Barlow Enterprises Facebook page now.

We'll follow you back!

CHAPTER 3

The Identity Question

Question 1: Who am I?

Your self-concept is an essential part of living a purposeful life. One component of your self-concept is your vision of your ideal-self. Your vision guides how you develop your character and shapes your personality.

In the Global Destiny Institute, the vision of your ideal-self is your written description of the person you imagine yourself becoming.

Don't be a slave to the opinions of others. Don't constantly worry about what others think about you. Instead of being controlled by the opinions of others, be controlled by your positive vision of yourself.

Who are you?

Name yourself. Reject disempowering labels such as poor, depressed, lazy, not good enough, and afraid. For a moment, reject even labels with positive connotations such as responsible, nurturing, provider, resourceful, multitalented, and giving. These labels are sometimes shrouded in pride or in other's perceptions or wishes for us and can therefore become seriously debilitating in our personal pursuit of authentic purpose.

Remember, a primary objective of this work is to equip you to think, write, and take strategic action toward living on purpose. So, how are you to proceed?

First of all, know that you have the power to shape your own identity. Second, think about and write down all of the characteristics, values, and traits that you want to exhibit. Third, take action!

Is it love, grace, joy, humor, courage, wealth, confidence and peace that you want to represent? Begin to think, live, look and act like the person who personifies those traits and before long you will become her. What's interesting is that as you imagine who you would like to become and set goals that move you closer to this ideal, your ideal-self evolves, and becomes an unstoppable catalyst for change in your life and in the lives of others.

One of the most difficult questions to answer is actually a question of purpose. Have you ever been at a loss for where to begin when asked, ***"Tell me about yourself****?"*

Of all the demands of culture and society, self-reflection is not usually one of them. Consequently, few people think very deeply, for extended times, on a consistent basis about their lives. At phases in our lives in which, we are preparing for a job or on a first date, few people can honestly answer a question like this.

Ideally, the fundamental questions would be asked, reflected upon, and written about progressively from childhood through adulthood. This way, long before we are old enough to think about choosing college majors, looking for work, dating, and making other critical life decisions, we'd possess a sound sense of who we are and could make choices that serve and support our identities.

Get Naked!

One of the best ways to answer this question is to focus on who you are outside the context of your business, your job, your school, and all of your extracurricular activities. It is difficult not consider your position at work or school or the various roles you play in relation to others, but in the interest of exposing your pure interests, try not think about yourself in terms of the titles you hold or the duties you perform. Do not think of yourself as Plumber, President, Construction Worker, CEO, Nanny, Executive Director, Cashier, Manager, Waitress, Pilot, Artist, Doctor, Bus Driver, Teacher, or whatever your profession. Do not think of yourself as father, mother, daughter, son, nephew, niece, or in terms of any other role or relationship that makes you consider who you are based on your perception of someone else's definitions, expectations, or demands of you. This is not easy, but it is possible.

Thinking in this way takes great courage and it takes time. It takes courage because to even position yourself to answer the question, challenges you to set aside the things that you so naturally do from day to day.

It also makes you face the fact that you may not be where you should or would have been if you had thought in this way sooner.

Honestly answering the question requires you to quiet yourself and strip; strip back the layers and layers of assumptions that you accept every day until you reach your bare soul -- where your true self lies. Imagine the *real you* sitting in a fetal position in anxious expectation as you peel back layers of life's assertions. Who were you really called to be?

> *Compared to what we ought to be, we are only half awake. We are making use of only a small part of our physical and mental resources. Stating the thing broadly, the human individual thus lives far within his limits. He possesses powers of various sorts which he habitually fails to use.*
>
> *~ Professor William James of Harvard*

What Matters is Who you Become on the Way to IT

It is not what you do. *It* is who you become. What's your *it*? When you **Check Your Heart,** pillar number one, what is *it* that constantly whispers to you from within to get started, continue, or complete *it*? When you see someone else doing *it* why do you think to yourself I can do *it* better than they? Why is it that every time you see *it* you cry and are compelled to fix *it*? Or why do you feel amazingly happy doing *it*?

We all have an *it*. *It* is that thing that you feel compelled to create, continue, complete, or do better than anyone you know.

Your *it* will require you to find a very quiet, still place in which you can be alone. We often teach in *Kings & Queens*, our relationship series, that *alone* is not a depressing, shameful word. On the contrary, we celebrate aloneness for couples and singles alike. Solitude is as much a human need as socializing with others. We dare say our world may be better if more of us understood how to transform alone time into times of reflection, healing, and peace and to use them as springboards from which we launch into our passions and purposes for life. To be alone is not a shame. Alone simply means to be all in one.

I (Jéneen) need you to absolutely tune in here because what I will share next is one of the most important lessons that I have ever learned in my life. As I shared earlier, I watched both my father and my mother take their last breaths as they transitioned from earth back home. I do not know of any sane person who has dealt with any aspect of death and remained the same. I certainly left each of my experiences with death forever changed. Thankfully, I also left with vital life-enriching lessons that will hopefully add light to your path too.

As I watched my loved ones dying and particularly after they had died, I realized that what mattered more than what they had accomplished, was who they had become.

The *it* – the goals, the dreams, the things for which they strived -- were merely results. But the character, the qualities, the lessons learned and transferred to me by my parents due to the processes they endured on the way to *it*, were what mattered much, much more than their final attainment of any particular goal or dream.

This truth applies to you. You have to spend time alone because in the grand scheme of things, in spite of all of the time, effort, money, and heart that you invest into accomplishing *it*, what will matter most, in the end, is not what you did, but *who you became in the process.*

Who are you?

This is the first of all the fundamental questions because it is not the number of degrees you hold, the tier of the university from which you graduated, how much you have traveled the world, or the wealth of experience that you bring from a particular field that will have the most lasting impact, positive or negative, on your professional and personal life. These things may carry you far for some time, but ultimately, your peace, your success and your legacy are predicated neither in what you've attained nor in what you have accomplished, but in the type of person you become.

Name You!

As a former faculty member at a university in a suburb of Pennsylvania, whenever I (Jéneen) taught Sociology and Business courses, one of the texts that I required for my students was Mr. Russell Simmons', *Do You! 12 Laws to Access the Power in You to Achieve Happiness and Success.*

Simmons, the co-founder of Def Jam records and Phat Farm, has a net worth of more than $340 million dollars. Needless to say, he is an extraordinary businessman and activist, yet his message, at its core, is not about how to amass billions of dollars. Of all that he could have shared, Mr. Simmons chose to tell us to identify, discover, and do what will enable you to find peace within. The real message of *Do You!* is spiritual. Law number 12 is, "Always do you." This, for him, means *"staying true to who you are and what you like instead of following trends."*

The task of learning and then staying true to who you are is required if you want to **Live on Purpose!** But before you can "Do You", you have to answer the question, Who am I? Once you answer this question, you have to do what every parent does when a new human being joins the world -- name them!

Sometimes we meet people who say, "I want to be a better person or I have a vision of embracing different qualities, but I just don't know how to change." The solutions are clear. Discover your purpose and potential, name yourself by writing down who you want to become, and begin to act-out the qualities that you seek to embody. Eventually, the acting out ends and in less time than you imagined, the you that you were pretending to be becomes the real you.

In essence, in order to become a better leader you must lead. In order to be loving and compassionate, you must do loving and compassionate things. The key is that you do not allow other people to define you. The key is that you strategically and consistently act in ways that demonstrate who you want to be.

Several years ago, while they were playing, our two oldest children, Grace and Joshua, reminded us of the importance of naming ourselves. During a typical moment of child's play, Josh was chasing Grace as she laughed a contagious belly laugh. Then she would chase him around and around the sofa until they both fell to the floor giggling and rolling about. In the midst of rolling and laughing Gracie said, "Joshy, let's play princess. I'll be the princess. Who will you be?" Josh hesitated. "Joshy," Grace repeated, "Who will you be?" Josh was distracted for some reason and he did not answer her. Frustrated and ready to move forward with playing princess she shoved him to the floor, climbed up on his back and proudly declared, "You will be my horse!" "No, no!" Josh cried, "I did not want to be the horse. I wanted to be the Prince." "Oh, well!" his sister carelessly replied.

What happened? For whatever reason, Joshua was distracted when Grace asked him who he wanted to be. He was not prepared with an answer so, ready to move on with her life, she gave him a name that he would not have given himself -- **horse**. When presented with the chance to tell the world who you are, be prepared. Exercise your authority and your responsibility over your destiny. Name *yourself.* If you don't, other people may do it for you.

Just ordinary words?

It has been said that we are what we eat. Another saying rings as true. You are what you speak. We explore the power of using your words without fear extensively in, *Don't Be Scared. BEspeak! How to Prepare, Present, and Inspire your Audience to Take Action.* One of my favorite passages is from chapter two, *Learn, Teach, Act, Speak* where I share the poignant reflection of the brilliant, late, Ms. Audre Lorde. Here is what Ms. Lorde wrote about the power of words:

> *I was going to die, sooner or later, whether or not I had even spoken myself. My silences had not protected me. Your silences will not protect you . . . What are the words you do not yet have? What are the tyrannies you swallow day*

by day and attempt to make your own, until you will sicken and die of them, still in silence? We have been socialized to respect fear more than our own need for language.

I began to ask each time: "What's the worst that could happen to me if I tell this truth?" Unlike women in other countries, our breaking silence is unlikely to have us jailed, "disappeared" or run off the road at night. Our speaking out will irritate some people, get us called bitchy or hypersensitive and disrupt some dinner parties. Our speaking out will permit other women to speak, until laws are changed, and lives are saved, and the world is altered forever.

Next time, ask: What's the worst that will happen? Then push yourself a little further than you dare. Once you start to speak, people will yell at you. They will interrupt you, put you down and suggest it's personal. And the world won't end.

And the speaking will get easier and easier. And you will find you have fallen in love with your own vision, which you may never have realized you had. And you will lose some friends and lovers, and realize you don't miss them. And new ones will find you and cherish you. And you will

> *still flirt and paint your nails, dress up and party, because, as I think Emma Goldman said, 'If I can't dance, I don't want to be part of your revolution.' And at last you'll know with surpassing certainty that only one thing is more frightening than speaking your truth. And that is not speaking.*

Words have unmistakable power. You can create and recreate reality with your words.

Because of the way we are designed, we have the ability to speak things into existence.

In *An Ordinary Man*, the riveting autobiography about the unthinkable and shameful 1994 genocide of the Rwandan people, Paul Rusesabagina reveals, with astounding simplicity and clarity, the creative influence of words. *"What,"* Rusesabagina asks desperately, *"had caused this to happen? Very simple,"* he concludes, *"Words."*

Of all that he experienced in his successful fight to create a safe haven for over one thousand Tutu and moderate Hutu refugees in the center of madness so atrocious it was surreal, Rusesabagina says,

This is what I want to tell you: Words are the most effective weapons of death in a man's arsenal. But they can also be powerful tools of life. They may be the only ones. Today I am convinced that the only thing that saved those 1,268 people in my hotel was words . . . Just ordinary words.

~ Paul Rusesabagina

By his own account, it was words that created the mayhem in Rwanda, and it was words that enabled him to save over a thousand precious lives. Quite simply, lives were both saved and destroyed by words. If, in a situation as grave as the Rwandan genocide, life can come by words, then surely you can use your words to transform your life, and the lives of those you are called to save, into lives of passion and purpose and you can make that happen with your ordinary words.

Who am I?

Over the years I (Omar) have literally taught thousands of students and every so often I have a chance to form a special relationship with a few of them. I had the fortune of getting to know a student named Nicole Horn. As is my custom with students I befriend, Ms. Horn met my wife and my children, and even attended a number of events at which Jéneen and I were the keynote speakers.

Over ten years ago, in the process of preparing their daughter for college, Nicole's parents hired my wife and me as Ms. Horn's Private Coaches. Nicole was one of our first Executive Partners. Recently, we had the pleasure of witnessing her marry an outstanding young man who was also my former student.

Nicole's parents scheduled a number of sessions and back then, the sessions were held in our home office. The first time Nicole visited our home, she was shocked. She could not believe what she saw (or what she didn't see). Upon entering my home, she discovered that I had no furniture in my living room. She had no idea that we had recently moved. She was shocked; she told everyone in her family.

Later, her mother told me what Nicole had said when she returned home. "Mom, I thought Mr. Barlow was rich; I didn't know that he was poor. He didn't have any furniture."

Here's the lesson. From the way I taught and presented myself at school, Nicole perceived that I was wealthy. I am. I was without furniture at that time, but I was simply waiting for my reality to catch up to my declarations. In the midst of waiting, I knew that even if our furniture-less home was in conflict with my student's perception of me, it was important for Nicole to discover that neither a home fully furnished, nor any material objects for that matter, informed my sense of identity. I was not depressed or sullen because I did not have certain things yet and I never saw myself as inferior which is why she didn't see me as inferior either. Rather, I believed that my identity was connected to my spirituality, my purpose, my history, and my family. So a home without furniture, one which she called "empty," had no bearing at all on how I conducted myself or on my self-image.

Today, I am proud to say that my home is beautifully furnished. People constantly compliment my humble abode. I smile and appreciate when they do, but I decided a long time ago not to allow material things to be a factor that defines who I am.

Decreeing & Becoming Who I Am

Nothing alive is static. Everything, including you, is in a constant state of change. This is why you never have to remain trapped where you are.

Let's imagine that you are poor and daily begin to declare, "I am rich." At the moment of your declaration, if it is sincere, you will begin to take responsibility for becoming rich. Of course, you will need a plan and you will need to work diligently but it is your declaration and your will to work that cause your plans to manifest.

At its source, this "I am" principle operates from the universal law of attraction and naming.

As children, we give others glimpses into who we really are but usually the clarity of our unencumbered younger selves gets stripped away. As a result, we find ourselves all grown up yet desperately searching for what we loved -- for who we were.

Our Nate is a perfect example. Nathanael, when he was two, often methodically marched about our home growling and swiping his little fat hands, turned paws, at us like he was a lion in the circus. He'd convincingly roar, "Me a dinosaur. No. No. Me a lion. Me gonna' get you. Rooaar!" Sometimes he would pretend, especially after we had returned from a speaking engagement or from worship, that he was the keynote speaker. He'd search for anything that would serve as a microphone, perch himself upon the windowsill of the bay window and begin to speak. Nate would walk back and forth, changing his intonations, smiling, walking, stopping, and posing. He'd work the crowd (usually Omar, me, and his hysterically laughing brother and sister) and he always welcomed our applause.

One Sunday we took Nathanael to prayer. Unaware of Nathanael's antics our pastor teasingly offered Nate the microphone. He excitedly grabbed the microphone and began to shout and speak. The audience of at least one thousand people exploded into laughter. Nate knew what he was doing. He garnered exactly the response he was looking for. He was being who he was. And he was proud.

As we age, things happen that chip away at the innocent, unapologetic bravado that most of us possess as children. This is unfortunate because as children, we give the most telling glimpses into our true identities. Observe children carefully. Take notes about the things they do and say. We keep journals for each of our children and as avid journalers ourselves, we encourage them to reflect and write and draw their dreams onto paper.

The late, brilliant businessman and internationally acclaimed speaker, Jim Rohn always said that it is our pictures, our journals, and our libraries that are life's most precious gifts. Write about your hopes, dreams, joys, challenges, and memories and record the precious things that you remember about what your children say and do as they grow. These prove to be rare and valuable treasures that your children will need and use as you all do the work necessary to help them cast off fear and Live on Purpose!

As Paul Rusesabagina reminds us,

Words are the most effective weapons of death in a man's arsenal. But they can also be powerful tools of life. They may be the only ones.

It takes courage to grow up and become who you really are.

~ E.E. Cummings

Reflect. Write. Share. Your words will provide the insight and the life needed to help you and your children declare with confidence. "I am!"

Come Out Now and Play

In *The Narrative of the Life of Frederick Douglass, An American Slave,* Douglass provides a quintessential example of the "I Am" concept. After being savagely beaten by his slave-master, Mr. Covey, Douglass writes that he decided that he would not be beaten again, and if anyone did decide to beat him, they would have to succeed in killing him. Though Douglass was not physically free, it is apparent that he decided in his mind that he would no longer be a slave. Hence, he boldly declares:

> *You have seen how a man [became] a slave; you shall see how a slave [became] a man . . . I re solved that, however long I might remain a slave in form, the day had passed forever when I could be a slave in fact.*

Frederick Douglass experienced "*becoming,*" and it was such an accomplishment because he did so under one of the most vicious and barbaric institutions in the history of the world -- American slavery. When freed from slavery, Douglass became an abolitionist and human rights advocate.

His life affirms how, by changing our state of mind and by changing what we say, we *can* change who we are.

When thinking about how important identity and of the power of words are, the work of another famous American author, the gifted Ralph Ellison comes to mind. The *Invisible Man* was published in 1952 and is still hailed as a masterpiece. The words of Ellison's main character in the novel are chilling. Concerning his identity, the narrator claims:

> *I am the invisible man. No, I am not a spook like those who haunted Edgar Allan Poe; nor am I one of those Hollywood-movie ectoplasms. I am a man of substance, of flesh and bone, fiber and liquids – and I might even be said to possess a mind. I am invisible understand because people refuse to see me. When they approach me they see only my surroundings, themselves, or figments of their imagination–indeed, everything and anything except me.*

Conscious of his invisibility to others, the nameless main character, if he is to survive, must come to terms with his own identity. In his quest to find and affirm his sense of self, the character fights the temptation to remain satisfied with the opinions of others. His words capture his painful struggle:

> *I've never been more loved and appreciated than when I tried to justify and affirm someone's mistaken beliefs. Too often, in order to justify them, I had to take myself by the throat and choke myself until my eyes bulged and my tongue hung out and wagged like the door of an empty house in a high wind. Oh, yes, it made them happy and it made me sick. There is by the way, an area in which man's feelings are more rational than his mind, and it is precisely in that area that his will is pulled in several directions at the same time.*
>
> *You might sneer at this, but I know now. I was pulled this way and that for longer than I can remember. And my problem was that I always tried to go in everyone's way but my own. I have also been called one thing and then another while no one wished to hear what I called myself. So after years of trying to adopt the opinions of others I finally rebelled. I am an invisible man.*

He finished his "I am" with invisible. But how do you choose to complete yours? Who do you say that you are? Complete the phrase. I am . . .

____

____

____

Interestingly the character's awareness of how he is perceived by others compels him to hide. He chooses to live underground in a basement and refuses to conform to the patterns that the world has set for him. Eventually, he returns to society, because he believes that *"humanity is won by continuing to play in the face of certain defeat."*

Most powerful is that the nameless character thinks deeply about what the world would lose without his presence. Take some time to think about that. What would the world lose without your presence? Without you, the world would be different. Ultimately, the main character decides to do what you have to do. He assumes his identity. May his words move you to do the same:

> *I'm shaking off the old skin and I'll leave it here in the hole. I'm coming out, no less in visible without it, but coming out nevertheless. And I suppose it's damn well time. Even hibernations can be overdone, come to think of it. Perhaps that's my greatest social crime; I've overstayed my hibernation, since there's possibility that even an invisible man has a socially responsible role to play.*

The world is waiting for you. Come out now and play!

> *I created the Freedom Sculpture because I knew that the struggle to be free was universal to the human condition.*
>
> *~ Zenos Frudakis*

The Destiny Seeker's Challenge

Reread the *Get Naked* section of this chapter. Think about your life. List all of the titles that you hold below. Include the roles that you operate in at home, work, school, your community, etc.

____

____

____

____

____

Now, look at your list again. Cross out every title that that does not support your vision of who you really are. Cross out every title that comes with roles and responsibilities that do not support who you want to become. People who are ultra-successful are ultra-focused. Your list should be much shorter now. Rewrite up to three titles you really want to keep:

____

____

____

____

____

Today, resign from at least three extracurricular activities or commitments that are not in synergy with your vision of who you are.

Cheryl Richardson, Life Coach and Author of ***Life Makeovers*** says, "A high quality life has more to do with what you remove from it, than what you add to it."

If your job is on the list, do not quit just yet! You need a strategic plan before you make that move.

Today I reclaim time that I should be giving to living my purpose by discontinuing my involvement in:

____

____

____

____

____

Share your progress! Tweet your what most challenged or inspired you from Chapter three, The Identity Question to @BeMorExcellent or post it on Barlow Enterprises Facebook page now.

We'll follow you back!

CHAPTER 4

The Source Question

Question 2: Where did I come from?

Your potential is only as great as your source.

You choose the sources from which you draw your energy, encouragement, and information. You have the responsibility to disconnect from every source that distracts or prohibits you from living your life on purpose.

The second of the five fundamental questions of life is, "Where did I come from?" This is a question of source. The question takes two primary sources into consideration:

1. **Your Spiritual Source**
2. **Your Ethnic Source**

Spiritual Source

Since I was about fifteen years old, I (Omar) have studied, thought and taught about purpose and destiny. My family, friends, students and audiences know that purpose is my major theme.

One morning while talking two of my dearest student-friends, Randolph and James, I came to understand an important aspect of purpose, on a much deeper, spiritual and emotional level than ever before.

The belief that human beings were designed by God and that God is the creator of everything are fundamental aspects of my philosophy of purpose. James, Randolph, and I were reading the story of Jeremiah. Jeremiah receives a message concerning his purpose in life and he is sent into a particular region to dispel several philosophies that the people in his native land have embraced. But, his response to the mission is not good. Jeremiah is terribly afraid. He emphatically rejects the mission because he believes that he is not equipped to fulfill the assignment. And Jeremiah had a lot of, what he thought were valid reasons, for why he could not move forward. His primary excuse was that he was too young. Nonetheless, God tells him not to be afraid and reminds Jeremiah that he will never leave him alone. God prefaces the call to purpose by saying,

Before I formed you . . . I knew you.

These seven words have enormous implications. Jeremiah's story suggests two things. First, it suggests that, he existed in some other place before he was born. Second, it explains that he was known *before* he was formed. Thus, the Source of this young man's life, and the Deliverer of the assignment, had detailed information about Jeremiah's reason for being, and his purpose, long before he was conceived and long before he was born.

Destiny Seed

Your purpose was established before you were.

- How could the fact that you were known before you were conceived change your attitude and benefit your life?

First of all, God was establishing the fact that He had information about Jeremiah's life and Jeremiah's ability (information that Jeremiah did not have) because God *knew* that Jeremiah would become fearful. He knew that he would begin to recite all of the inadequacies that he had. He knew that if Jeremiah played those negative affirmations over and over in his consciousness that it would stop him from doing what he was supposed to do.

Destiny Seed

Regardless of whether they ever tell you (and most will not) people can sense your greatness.

By telling Jeremiah that He was known before, God positions Himself as the authority, silences Jeremiah's excuses, and quiets his fears. Most significantly, He implies that He knows, in spite of Jeremiah's self-doubt, that Jeremiah can handle the challenges he will face.

Similarly, whether it is a parent, a supervisor, a child, a partner, a client, or a desire from your heart that calls on you to do something great, if you are asked to accomplish a particular task, it means that it was perceived, *before* you were approached, that you can handle it.

You have what it takes to deliver on the request.

Secondly, if you believe that your life, and the contributions that will flow from your life to change the lives of others, was established in a time and space that preceded your conception, you will benefit in at least two ways.

First, you will understand that both you and your assignment have been carefully considered, planned for, and completed -- before you started stressing out about it.

Second, belief that a Source greater than you already knew and had good plans for your life, allays fear. By believing that it was already established, you get to relax. Believing in this way triggers your self-conscious to think, *"If my purpose was established before, then in spite of the great fear and uncertainty that I have at times, I must possess everything that I need to move forward and to succeed."*

If, on the day you were born, your purpose in life was already established that means that in spite of your mistakes, you can fulfill your purpose.

Why?

Destiny Seed

What you have to offer never depended upon you being perfect. Your ability to be a gift to the world was settled before you were born. What you have to do is Keep Moving Forward.

Consequently what you do after you are born does not change what you were assigned to do before you born.

As an instructor, I (Jéneen) prepare my students' assignments before the semester begins. Everything they have to do is written in their syllabus. Before they meet me in person, before I know their names, faces, or skill levels, before they receive grades, before they even learn the content that I have to teach, I assign them tasks. I plan strategically so that those who do the work benefit. We all know ahead of time what the outcomes of the course are and can easily measure whether those outcomes are achieved.

Everyone begins with the same grade and everyone has the opportunity to complete their assignments. If students decide not to complete assignments, their decision does not change the fact that the assignments were prepared before the course began and that the assignments are due at the course's end.

Similarly, your purpose is established and you are responsible to complete your assignment.

Choose Your Well, Well

In the process of answering the question, "Where did I come from?" we consider both your spiritual source and your ethnic source. As it relates to your spiritual source, understanding a few things about *wells* offers great insight.

There are basically three types of *wells*. Wells can be dug, driven, or drilled but all wells serve the function of providing clean water for people, irrigation, and industries. Your spiritual source is your primary life-sustaining source.

Often, tragedies and trials serve as two of the greatest revealers of one's source in life. For instance, on September 11, 2001 the United States experienced one of the worst attacks on its land since Pearl Harbor Day on December 7, 1941. The World Trade Center's towers, nearly 100 stories, were shockingly reduced to dust and rubble as a result of being hit by two planes. Over 2,500 people lost their lives in those buildings and 184 were instantly killed when American Airlines Flight 77 crashed into The Pentagon.

No amount of money could heal the pain of the people who endured these strikes. Business networks and contacts were virtually useless due to the attack and it did not take long at all for people to realize that they needed sources other than money, power, prestige, status, family, education, self and other sources on which people naturally and steadily rely. People began to pray. In fact, on September 14, 2001, President George W. Bush called the nation to prayer. At the height of power, even the President recognized that our nation was in desperate need of help that was greater than he.

In our quest to inspire, educate and equip people to live lives of excellence, we teach, speak to, and consult for various industries and for people of all nations, creeds, classes, and faiths. One of the things that our audiences say they love about us is the evidence that we are very well read and that we exhibit genuine love and respect for one another and for others. People frequently ask about our spiritual source. We don't mind sharing that we highly value simplicity, laughing out loud, and living with honesty and integrity. We take seriously the disciplines of meditation, prayer, and service to the least of those among us. Jesus Christ is *our* source.

> *If you want to know the purpose of a thing, never ask the thing. A created thing can never know what was in the mind of the creator when he planned and built it.*
>
> ~ *Myles Munroe*

What is your spiritual source? Even if it is different from ours, in order to live on purpose you need to identify and consistently connect to your spiritual source.

Let's consider some other relevant facts about wells. When water levels fall below the level of the pump's intake, wells begin to pump air and then run dry. We can all learn essential lessons from this characteristic of wells.

Destiny Seed

Avoid being a person that is, as the saying goes, full of hot air. Don't run dry! Monitor what you take in. Keep your spirit filled with excellent things.

As pursuers of a more excellent life we want to be sure that we are full of life giving water, not air. Since living on purpose will inevitably lead to touching the lives of others, you definitely cannot afford to run dry. So, let your spiritual choice be reflected in your heart and *especially* in your habits because it is not what you get that matters most. What matters most, is who you become.

Destiny Seed

Be wise. Do not wait for tragedy and trial to force you into deciding upon your spiritual source.

Begin to reflect upon what you believe and in whom you believe now. And in the process of deciding, remember: The greater your source, the greater your potential.

Ethnic Source

> *We are so ignorant of our back history. We are very busy with our own lives [yet] we are the sum of all the people who have lived before us.*
>
> *~ Meryl Streep*

As we continue to study the second of the five fundamental questions of life, "Where did I come from?" it is as essential to clarify your spiritual source as it is to understand, acknowledge, and appreciate your ethnic source.

As a former teacher at North Penn High School (Omar), one of my favorite student projects was our Ethnic Research and Poster assignment. Before assigning the task, I would give my students an impassioned speech about the importance of understanding and taking pride in one's heritage. I taught predominantly Caucasian students: "You're not white!" I would bellow dramatically as I slowly paced the floor. I'd look serious and sure. My "white" students looked confused and surprised. They'd go home and tell their parents, "Hey, today Mr. Barlow told me that I was not white." "Yeah," they told me their parents would reply. "Then what are you?"

Year after year, my students and I would laugh together about the speech and about their parents' initial reply to the students' partial telling of my speech. They rarely told their parents the whole story but everyone eventually got to see our point as we decorated the class with amazing displays of our rich cultures, conducted interviews and wrote in-depth papers about our ethnic sources.

We would laugh together at their initial responses to, "You're not White!" Before long I'd glory in watching the lights in their minds click and their countenances brighten as I'd continue, "You are Italian. You are Greek. You are Irish. You are . . . "

The PBS documentary, *Faces of America,* with scholar Henry Louis Gates, Jr., underscores the essentiality of knowing from where we come. As he has done in his other special, African American Lives, the Harvard University professor uses genealogy and genetics to uncover the histories of twelve renowned Americans. Famous person after famous person we witness the impact that discovering where we come from has on our lives. Thankfully, technology and science have enabled us to reply with accuracy and ethnic pride to the question, "Where did I come from?"

> *If they could do that with nothing, what can I do I can fly."*
>
> ~ *Oprah Winfrey*

Destiny Seed

Know your source. And be proud.

The BE Challenge:

List the first two fundamental questions below:

What is your spiritual source?

What is your ethnic source?

We love hearing from you. Share your progress! Tweet what most challenged or inspired you from Chapter four, The Source Question, to @BeMorExcellent or post it on Barlow Enterprises Facebook page now. We'll follow you back!

CHAPTER 5

The Purpose Question

Question 3: Why Am I Here?

This is the true joy in life, the being used for a purpose recognized by yourself as a mighty one; the being thoroughly worn out before you are thrown on the scrap heap; the being a force of nature instead of a feverish selfish little clod of ailments and grievances complaining that the world will not devote itself to making you happy.

~ George Bernard Shaw

There are a number of purpose sub-questions that will assist you in discovering your purpose. These questions force you to think through who you are and what you really want to do in your life. The goal of *Don't Be*

Scared. Live On Purpose! is to provide you with a process that you can use to understand how to think, write, and act in ways that enable you to live your more excellent life.

When you contemplate and write down your responses to these questions you are training your mind to disregard limiting thoughts and to take full advantage of the possibilities that lie in wait for your life. In chapters three and four we studied the questions of identity and source. Now, we will explore one of our favorite questions of the fundamental five, **Why am I here?** This is a question of purpose.

Destiny Seed

Destiny Seekers define purpose or mission as your written down reason for being.

What you need in order to discover and live on purpose is already within you. That is why, in chapter two, we discussed asking excellent questions so that you receive excellent answers.

As you prepare yourself to read this chapter:

Read with your pen in hand.

- **Go to place where you can be alone for a few moments to read and take notes.**

- **Prepare your mind for a barrage of propelling questions.**

Expect to gain clarity from this process.

This chapter is an invitation to join fellow Destiny Seekers on an exciting journey to clarity. Imagine yourself as a shelled mollusk. Sometimes in the process of trying to find out or to refine who we are and what we should be doing with our lives we can feel as insignificant and invisible as a mollusk in its shell. When a mollusk experiences an attack from the outside or when something such as sand, parasites, or some other irritant enters the shell of a mollusk, the creature creates a sac to ward off the irritation. As we know, what began as an attack from outside or as an irritation from within sparks a process that creates a magnificent pearl!

Similarly, when we are bombarded with the demands of marriage, children, work, school, romance and the many other challenges of life, nature and time have a way of transforming circumstances that begin as irritating nuisances into stunning, priceless gems.

The chapter is designed to penetrate the "shells" on your mind and heart and to nudge you from your comfort zones by hurling a myriad of questions at you. We want to infiltrate the cozy places of your life. We want you to experience the benefits of answering some of the questions of purpose. It can be a daunting process, but living with the peace and excitement of knowing that you are doing exactly what you were born to do does not come cheaply. As my mother-in-love, Mrs. Evelyn Barlow, says:

Destiny Seed

Purpose does not happen by chance; it happens by choice.

Let Life Begin

> *Life begins with questions. Nothing shapes our lives as much as the questions we ask, or refuse to ask.*
>
> *~ Richard Leider*

To help you to warm-up to this idea of answering questions, by both contemplating and writing, and eventually by posing essential life questions to yourself, we present you with three scenarios. Take about ten minutes to read and write your answers for at least one of the three questions. Time yourself and focus. Allow your mind and heart to relax. *Dream. Be Free.* The goal right now is simply to get started, not to finish, so don't pressure yourself. There are three scenarios. Read them all then choose to answer the questions from at least one of them.

Choose your favorite. Write for about twenty minutes, then move on. You will come back to the scenarios as many times as you need to later on. Have fun!

Scenario #1

Imagine and Write (Be specific): Congratulations! You just won ten million, tax free, dollars!

- **What will you do differently?**
- **What is the first change you will make in your life?**
- **What will you start doing that you are not doing right now?**
- **What will you stop doing?**
- **With unlimited time and resources, what kind of work will you choose to do?**

- **Who will you decide not to allow in your circle anymore? Why are you disconnecting from them?**
- **Should you change who is in your circle of friends based on your responses to this scenario? Explain.**

Scenario #2

Imagine and Write (Be specific): Everyone in the labor market is paid $10 an hour, regardless of the type of work performed. Janitors earn the same as lawyers; doctors the same as artist; presidents and chief executives the same as customer service representatives, rabbis, authors, scientists or nannies. The same amount of power, prestige, and status are given to all positions. You have the time and intelligence to do whatever you desire and you will receive the education and the money you need to become skilled at whichever profession you choose.

- **Which profession will you choose?**
- **Specifically why did you choose that profession?**
- **How will you feel doing this type of work?**
- **Do you experience any of those feelings in your current work or volunteer experiences?**

- **Is the work you do now related in any way to what you would do if money and status were not an issue? How?**
- **Specifically what factors led you to choose the field you are in now?**
- **If you are not working in a position that energizes and excites you, what steps could you take to move into a more fulfilling line of work?**

Scenario #3

Imagine and Write (Be specific):

You are ninety years old. You have just received a contract to write your life story. Both a book and a movie will be produced by a major production agency.

What will your autobiography highlight about your life?

- **What are the major themes of your book?**
- **What kind of person did you become?**
- **How would you describe your habits, morals and relationships with others?**
- **Write the eulogy that will be read at your funeral.**

- **How do you want to be remembered by the most important people in your life?**

Purpose Speaks

Your purpose is constantly speaking to you, nudging you about what to do and what not to do, who to call, who to avoid and what to create. Let's revisit our Destiny Statement™ Institute's *Four Pillars of Purpose*, from chapter one.

Pillars one and two, **Check your Heart** and **Dive Deep**, remind us that purpose is already very close to us. Where is it? The proverb says,

> *Purpose in the heart of man is like deep water, but a man of understanding will draw it out.*

So, purpose is in your heart. In addition to knowing that your purpose is in your heart, it is essential to **Seek Understanding**, pillar number three, so that you, or those who choose to mentor you, can dive deep enough to draw out the goodness and the answers that lie within you. Finally, you will experience the freedom, peace, and joy of the last pillar when you achieve **Flow** in your personal and professional life.

How Purpose Speaks

Purpose questions help to answer the question, Why am I here?

We have selected seven of our audiences' favorite questions of purpose. By answering more pointed, specific questions like the sub-questions of purpose, you will begin to chisel away at the overwhelming and more difficult task of answering the fundamental question, "Why am I here?"

Your purpose is close to you. It is in your heart and it speaks to you in the following ways:

Whose problems can you solve?

Whether I (Jéneen) am teaching sociology or business classes at the university, writing, speaking, coaching, or leading seminars, I have learned that helping students and professionals to pause and at least write a mission statement for their lives lays a solid foundation from which we can build a plan to help them reach their goals. The act of pausing to say, "You have a purpose in life, and I have an exercise that will help you begin to discover or clarify that purpose," stuns people. A very successful client stopped me in our initial strategy session and said, "Wait, a personal mission statement. Yes. That's exactly what I need. I just didn't know it!"

You add value to others when you can solve their problems. Whose problems can you solve?

Asking is the beginning of receiving. Anthony Robbins said,

> *The main difference between people who seemed successful in any area and those who weren't was that successful people asked better questions and as a result, they got better answers.*
>
> *~ Anthony Robbins*

<u>Destiny Seed</u>

The better questions you ask the better answers you will get. The better answers you get the better solutions you will find.

Think about it. The problem that most infuriates you is often an indication to your purpose. When you make a commitment to solving problems, some amazing things will begin to happen in your life. The problems you solve determine how you will be remembered. The problems you solve position you for friendship with uncommon leaders. The problems you solve cause people to see you as distinct from others. The problems you solve cause you to become the topic of discussion among people who need you to solve their problems. The problems you solve determine how much money you have the capacity to earn.

You are a solution.

Whose problems are you here to solve?

____

____

____

____

____

What would you do if you had no fear?

To this question some cynics reply that they would die if they had no fear. They reason that to live without fear is to live without inhibitions and that living without inhibitions can lead to death. Our goal here is not to unpack convoluted arguments or to counter the claims of cynics. The heart of the question, *"What would you do if you had no fear?"* is not intended to encourage carelessness. On the contrary, the question is an invitation to you to let your guard down. When you begin to think about what you would do if you had no fear you instantly position yourself to attract boundless opportunities.

As Diane Conway, the author of What would you do if you had no Fear: Living your Dreams While *Quakin' in Your Boots*, rightly claims, *"Asking and answering the question produces a divine flash that sets in motion assistance from out of the blue."*

At some level, you are somewhat aware of what you would do with your life if you were fearless. Subconsciously, however, fear stops you from taking the risks and actions necessary. Sometimes, you are as afraid of failing as you are of having wild success.

Liberate your mind so that you can move forward. **"What would you do if you had no fear?"**

List three things that you would do if you had no fear:

____

____

____

____

____

What grieves or hurts you enough for you to take action?

I (Jéneen) was listening to a training in my car. "The average accumulation of wealth among African Americans," the trainer said, "is $4500." I was driving and although it had happened to me one time before when I was studying statistics for a project of mine during my graduate schooling in Economic Development, I just was not prepared for it to happen to me again. I exhaled deeply in disgust. Then, I started to cry. Why did the statistic make me cry? I did not hear the statistics as just numbers. People whose hearts do not connect with solving this problem of generational economic despair only hear fours, fives, and zeros. But it's different for me. I hear the numbers, but in my mind's eye, I see the people. And I hurt over what that number means for the day to day lives of hundreds of thousands of men, women, and children. I am compelled to do something to help. This is how purpose speaks to your heart.

Do you care deeply about some person, cause, or situation? You care because you are supposed to do something to help heal the hurt.

Destiny Seed

Caring qualifies you as an instrument of healing.

Tears talk. Whatever grieves you is a clue to something that you are assigned to heal. Pay attention to your tears. You have to think about the things that you are extremely passionate about. For example, you may be moved by issues such as homelessness, poor education, poverty, financial indebtedness, domestic violence, or about persons who struggle with managing their time. But here is the key that separates Destiny Seekers from the masses. We think, not just about things for which we have passion, but we know exactly what causes, people groups, and challenges spark our passion to the degree that we are actually compelled to do something.

What hurts you enough for you to make a phone call now, volunteer for that cause, donate online, purchase the ticket, travel there to help, write a letter, finish the book, or make a visit to fill the need?

Talk is Cheap

If you are not moved to action, then you are not serious enough about that cause. You may be affected by numerous hurtful situations in our world but, remember our assignment in this book is to get you to think, write, *and* take action. Do not judge yourself if you come up with many things that are hurtful to you but for which you are not compelled to do something.

This is where having a coach becomes a serious asset to getting you to your next level. Your mind will default to creating reasons (excuses) for why you can't take action on the issue. That is normal. Expect it. But know that your passion for a cause or group of people will always override that initial resistance.

Let's think again about our *Four Pillars of Purpose*. For this sub-question of purpose, you really have to *Check Your Heart* and *Dive Deep*. What we are digging for is that thing that compels you to move out of your comfort zone.

In the process of writing this book, we presented the *Four Pillars of Purpose* to a group of young, professional parents and helped them all write personal mission statements. The audience also served as a focus group for our revised guide to writing your statement.

Everyone received the process extremely well, offered valuable feedback, and even asked that we come to present again because they wanted more of their friends and family to benefit from the workshop. One of my favorite comments came from a non-profit executive. After a few minutes of reading through the very comprehensive list of charities in the guide she looked up said, "Wow, after reading this list, I feel so selfish!" Of course we did not mean to make anyone feel selfish; her comment helped us to see that sharing the list does accomplish what we hoped it would. Sometimes, we just don't realize the hundreds of thousands of new, meaningful options and opportunities that exist for us to help others. The list that we shared encouraged her to broaden her perspective on how she could share her gifts and skills to serve others!

To download your free *Don't Be Scared. Live on Purpose! Destiny Statement™ Guide* to Writing Your Personal Mission Statement visit www.destinystatement.com

What hurts you enough to make you take action? List your answers below.

____

____

____

What do you hate?

Whatever you hate is a clue to something that you are called to correct. Think about it. Has something ever made you so angry that you said something like, "I wish that I could just . . ." or "I should have said . . ." Of course you have. It happens to all of us. Sometimes we are taught to as quickly as possible dismiss or get rid of feelings of anger.

Omar and I recommend that Destiny Seekers do exactly the opposite. The next time you feel angry, pause and examine why you are feeling angry. So many times, the incidences that provoke you to anger are the strongest ways in which purpose speaks to your heart. Being sensitive to things that make you angry helps you to discover your passion and purpose in life.

Love Speaks Through Anger

Anger can be one of the first signs that something you love has been violated. Author Timothy Keller explains how anger is the result of love when he writes,

> *Anger is the result of love. It is energy for defense of something you love when it is threatened. If you don't love something at all, you are not angry when it is threatened. If you love something a little, you get a little angry when it is threatened. If something you love is an 'ultimate concern,' if it is something that gives you meaning in life, then when it is threatened you will get uncontrollably angry.*

The next time that you feel angry, don't rush yourself into a state of calm before you explore whether purpose is speaking to you.

I (Jéneen) am a relatively calm person:

- I hate disingenuous behavior.
- I hate to see people in pain (especially children).
- I hate to see people confused about how to make their dreams happen.

When we think in terms of anger surfacing as the result of something we love, it makes perfect sense. Watch what happens when we change the statements above and state them in the positive.

- I love genuine behavior.

- I love to see people (especially children) happy.
- I love helping people gain clarity and take action on their dreams.

Now, let's test our "love speaks through anger" assertion again by looking at what I (Omar) love.

- I hate to see people fail to take advantage of life's possibilities.
- When people allow themselves to be ignorant, I hate it.
- I hate when people put forth no effort to; I hate when people won't even try.

Without a doubt, Omar is a world-class motivational speaker and educator. I am his wife and I listen to his CDs and videos over and over again. I mean that's just how powerful an educator and speaker he is. He has an unusual gift for moving people from not knowing, to understanding and being able to apply the information in ways that change their lives. He inspires people to learn more on their own. His love for seeing people live up to their potential has possessed him to spend countless hours, years, and resources studying how to usher people into life's possibilities.

When we translate what Omar hates into what he loves it sounds like this:

- I love to see people take advantage of life's possibilities.
- I love when people pursue knowledge.
- I love helping people to put forth their best effort.

Let's do this together now. **What do you hate?**

____

____

____

____

____

____

____

Now rewrite the things you hate as ***things that you love***:

____

____

____

____

____

____

____

What are you willing to trade your life (time) for?

Waste your money and you're only out of money, but waste your time and you've lost a part of your life.

~Michael LeBoeuf

I (Jéneen) passionately challenge people to "be clearer about your passions and your plans." You can hardly ever leave an event of mine without hearing me say, "Clarity is power! The clearer you become, the more powerful you become."

Destiny Seed

For Destiny Seekers, the words time and life are synonymous.

From now on, when you make decisions about how you spend your time, be conscious that you are actually making a decision about how you will spend a piece of your life – a piece of your life that you will never, ever be able to reclaim.

A very sharp gentleman who was an Executive Partner of ours comes to mind that I mentioned earlier in the book. Raphael was a very successful professional in one of the top three most lucrative industries in the world. He'd trained with the world-renowned peak performance coach, Mr. Anthony Robbins and had even successfully mastered Robbins' fire-walks. Raphael had studied and trained with hosts of others who are among the very best in the industry of personal development. Simply put, this gentleman was an elite professional who highly valued personal development. Raphael hired us as his personal coaches and we began to walk alongside one another because he had come to a place, as many successful people do, at which he needed to reassess what his next steps should be.

After just three, very productive sessions, Raphael said that he was "rejuvenated." He said that he was dreaming audaciously again. He had remembered and began to work towards some of his deepest heart's desires. I (Jéneen) noticed that Raphael's voice was alive again. He actually sounded like a new man. One day, our session was almost to a close and we were celebrating because we'd peeled back so many of what I call, life layers, that we'd rediscovered one of his truest passions. We had even planned what actions he would take before our next session. Then Raphael asked me a question that I did not expect. "One more thing," he said. "Because of my expertise in my field, I was asked to develop and direct this program. What do you think I should do?" "Well," I said to him, "in light of what has happened in today's session, let me ask you, how will you're doing this move you closer the dream we just rediscovered?" He was clear. "It will not," he said. "Okay," I responded, "How much closer will you be to the realization of your dream if you put your time (life) into taking the actions towards the dream instead of towards designing that program?" He acknowledged that he would be considerably closer to his dream. "Let's think about this then, Raphael." I continued, "Why, are we considering saying yes to the invitation to build that program?"

His answer held the key to why so many talented, successful people are stuck! I will never forget his tone as he slowly and hesitantly replied, "Well, because they need help and . . . because I can help." That was it. It was revolutionary. No more questions needed. I had questioned my friend into his own light. Although he could easily design and direct the program and help many by doing so, the program had nothing to do with Raphael's passion -- *nothing*. I would not tell him what to do, but I did question him into a space into which he could make the decision about how to trade his time (life) for himself.

Destiny Seed

Destiny Seekers make careful, deliberate decisions about how we invest our time. Consequently, we know when to say yes. We know when to say no. And we unapologetically answer requests made of our time with whichever reply is required.

This is the difference between those who fulfill their dreams and those who remain drifting dreamers. Many of the things that you are very good at and do comfortably are good, but are they are not activities that will make your dream a reality.

STOP SPENDING YOUR LIFE (YOUR TIME) ON THINGS THAT ARE NOT CONNECTED TO YOUR LIFE'S MISSION!

You need to take it as seriously as the old commercial that warned about the danger of taking drugs. When deciding how you invest your time, make that decision based upon how much closer the actions will be that move you towards your dream. If the answer is not much closer, then, ***"Just say, No!"***

Otherwise, you live drugged -- drug from this meeting to that meeting, drug into assignments that do not interest you, drug into relationships with people you really don't like being around, and the list goes on. Stop. Think. Decide, based on your life's purpose, and respond accordingly. Say no to being drugged!

Besides considering what types of work you spend your time on, here are a few other questions to consider. Who are the people you find yourself voluntarily getting together with again and again for deeper discussions? What types of things do friends, family members, colleagues or others consistently ask you to do? Are you clear about your mission? Do you make decisions about how to spend your time based on how the activity will move you toward your mission?

Name three activities that drain your energy and time:

____

____

____

____

____

____

____

> *Time is the most precious element of human existence. The successful person knows how to put energy into time and how to draw success from time.*
>
> *~ Dennis Waitley*

Money is not an issue. What type of work will you do?

This is definitely one of my (Jéneen) favorite questions! This question really cuts to the core of what it means to live on purpose. This question silences all of the nonsense in your heart and in your brain. It is an in your face, either tell me the truth or just don't pretend like you want to live your more excellent life type question.

Destiny Seed

Destiny does not discriminate. Clarity is a master key. Without it you will never unlock your destiny.

People from every socioeconomic status have to grapple with this question of purpose. Frankly, our friends, mentors, and clients who are in the top four percent of the nation's most wealthy individuals grapple with this question more deeply than most, because when you have extraordinary wealth, the question is more than an exercise.

Do not be fooled. The wealthy that live without a deep and enduring sense of purpose are among the most frustrated, reckless, and depressed people among us. The question, *How can I have so much and still feel so empty*? haunts many missionless multimillionaires.

It is okay to make a lot of money. And if you want to, we absolutely believe that you can and therefore you should. It is essential to remember that money has to be a means to a purposeful end. Money alone, does not promise fulfillment; but living on purpose always will.

Destiny Seed

Truly knowing your life's purpose is life's great equalizer. Truly knowing your life's purpose is the only thing that will really set you free.

Money is not an issue. What type of work you will do?

____

____

____

____

Let's Go "There"

Relax your mind and your body. Breathe intentionally. Breathe deep, cleansing breaths. Play music if it helps you to focus and relax. You are relaxed and you are free. You have all of the money you could possibly have. You buy anything you want to buy for yourself and for others. You travel anywhere you want to travel, with whomever you choose, and stay as long as you please. You do not want for anything. Still, you must choose to do some sort of work. Money is not an issue at all for you.

What kind of work will you do? Free your mind. See yourself there doing the work, excited by the work, fulfilled by and enjoying the work or what you know will come of it. How do you feel?

When you find yourself working on something, or with someone, and you do not even realize how quickly time has passed, you have achieved flow.

Can you recall a time in your life when you were in flow?

Were you painting? Were you traveling? Were you in the studio? Were you giving, serving, or speaking? Perhaps you were writing, dancing, thinking deeply or engaged in some inspiring conversation. How did the place look, smell, and feel? What was the weather? Were you alone or with others? Precisely what about that experience caused you to lose track of time? Write it down. Be as specific as possible. No detail is too insignificant.

The goal is for you to identify and then recreate those experiences over and over again. When you continuously clarify, visualize, and recreate these moments, you will more easily find ways to repeat those moments.

Destiny Seed

More Excellent Moments lead to More Excellent Days. More Excellent Days lead to More Excellent Months. More Excellent Months lead to More Excellent Years. More Excellent Years eventually and undoubtedly lead YOU into Your More Excellent Life!

Several years ago we were speaking at a national conference in Virginia that hosted thousands of secondary and higher educational professionals along with their most accomplished student leaders. The conference, founded and hosted by The Stuart Educational Leadership Group, was the life's work of one of our most beloved and respected mentors and friends, the late Dr. Carroll F.S. Hardy.

Dr. Hardy was also the former Associate Vice President of Student Affairs at the College of William and Mary. Like many of her "children," we lovingly called her Dean. For a decade, Dean invited us to speak at her annual conference. It was an honor. We certainly owe a great deal of the experience that we gained a speakers and trainers to Dr. Hardy.

She'd always say, "Now you know I can't pay you what you're worth to do this for these children!" We'd all laugh. Dean always took care of us in more ways than one, and although she always said it was not enough, she compensated us very well too. But even if Dean could not pay for our services, we knew that this was the work that we would do for free. Dean Hardy's annual invitation to speak at her conference afforded us opportunities to speak annually at many universities and events nationally. Not only that, but the preparation, sacrifice, and work that we put into preparing to speak at the conference each year, helped us ***to master our message***. We found ***flow*** both in the preparation and in the presentation.

Most of all, the consistent study, writing, planning and development of Barlow Enterprises, especially for the Destiny Statement™ Process, was incubated and refined during those years. Every year, we were inspired by the leaders' requests to hear more from us and by the students and administrators who packed our sessions out year after year. Every year the audiences would challenge us by asking, "Omar and Jéneen, where's your book!" Today, we are delighted to have authored two books and to announce to our audience, using the phrase we'd all chant together after we had presented, that several more books are "*Coming Soon!*"

It is paramount that you figure out what types of work you would do for free.

Stop Being Afraid. Just Get Started!

She was all the way in the back of the room. Our eyes met and she was speaking, without speaking to me, the way people do when their hearts are truly moved while they are listening to your talk. "What?" I asked her, "What would you do for free?" She did not hesitate, "I would make greeting cards." The audience made an audible and choir-like, "Awh" as if they were longing to read her cards. There was a girl next to her. She had the look too. Omar got to her with the microphone. "What would you do?" "I would play my guitar on the street and sing." She said. She looked relieved to have heard herself admit it aloud. Incredible! Another man said, "I want to work to eliminate corruption in the political system in my country, but where I am from, my parents say that I must become a doctor. So, I am a pre-med major."

What! Why aren't these people *doing* these amazing things? Wouldn't sharing their gifts add more beauty to our world, touch people's hearts, and help them to live in the peace and freedom that they deserve?

Why aren't you?

This is not a dress rehearsal! You only have one life to live. Get clear about your mission and vision in life. Make a plan of action. Get started. Move towards more excellent moments, days, weeks, months and years. Be courageous. It will not be easy. But we guarantee you . . . it will be worth it!

Who is doing what you would love to do?

Experience is *not* the best teacher.

> *The quickest way to grow and learn is through mentorship instead of through your mistakes. Experience is the slowest way of learning. Learning through mistakes will give you many, many setbacks. You could easily lose four or five years if you don't learn information the proper way because that knowledge is critical to your success.*
>
> ~ *Dr. Mike Murdock*

You have access to people who are doing what you would love to do with your life. Reach out to them. If you have not already identified and made a list of these individuals, don't worry. Think. Begin to identify them.

You know that you have found the caliber of people you need in your life when something inside of you leaps when you see them using their gifts. Sometimes you'll say to yourself, "I can do that." or "That's what I should be doing." Even more telling is when you see someone doing what you would love to do or what you should be doing and you say to yourself, "I can do that way better than they can!"

For instance, as educators, business people and professional speakers we have the books, CDs, and DVDs of thousands of teachers, speakers, researchers, and others who represent, in some way, what we love doing. Because we are committed to living More Excellent Lives, our libraries not only include the work of those in our line of work, but we have the materials of individuals from every single one of the seven key areas of life that we teach. Our library represents the many interests of our lives. We read, listen to and watch the works of painters, dancers, educators, runners, parents, business people, musicians, world leaders, travelers, intellectuals, philanthropists, and the list goes on. By intentionally exposing ourselves to vast subjects of study that are related to our passions and purpose, we glean wisdom and inspiration for our own lives and work. As you consider who is doing what you would love to do, here are several other questions you should ask yourself.

- Who do you admire or envy for the way they have applied their talents?
- Who is actually doing what you would love to do?
- How are you like these people? How are you unique?

- What can you learn from seeing the way they have lived purposefully?
- How can you save yourself time, money and energy by avoiding some of the mistakes they have made?
- Have you studied their teaching, purchased their materials, and applied what they share to your journey?
- Have you reached out to any of them with your compliments, gratitude and/or questions?

Mentors are not necessarily meant to be cheerleaders. They are the people who are willing to tell you what you do not want to hear. Swallow your pride. Humble yourself and position yourself to listen, learn, and implement the time (life) saving information that you will glean from your mentors.

If you intend to become who you were meant to become and to live the more excellent life that you deserve to live, you will invest your time and money into acquiring mentorship and coaching, and you will learn to become, what a treasured mentor of ours, Dr. Mike Murdock, calls a world-class protégé.

Save Your Life!

Several business partners and I had the pleasure of sharing a meal with another one of our mentors and friends. I asked, "Mr. Donalson, knowing all that you know now about building successful businesses, what one thing would you do differently?" He barely hesitated at all then said, "I would have asked for more help, and sooner."

In essence, he said the very same thing as Dr. Murdock. Mr. Donalson said that he would have saved himself years had he simply asked for more help faster. This is precisely why we dedicated an entire chapter, Chapter 2 to asking questions. Remember this acronym for ASK: Ask, Seek, Knock and do as the words advise. When you do, doors of incredible opportunity will be opened for you.

Destiny Seed

Everyone who asks receives. Everyone who seeks eventually finds. Ask. Seek. Knock. Do not stop until you get what you came for. Look for what you are supposed to give and give with grace, excellence, and all your might!

As the saying goes, time is money. That is true. Even more, as Destiny Seekers, be highly conscious of this fact: If time is valued because the loss of it means the loss of money, then how much more should you value your time?

Your time is your life. Consequently, when you use your time you are using your life. You can regain your money. You can never get your time back! Invest it wisely by identifying, observing, studying, and surrounding yourself with extraordinary mentors.

Who is doing what you would love to do?

____

____

____

____

____

The BE Challenge

You reflected and wrote a lot in this chapter. Congratulations for making this investment to gain clarity about your life! Simply go back and reread your notes from this chapter.

Based on everything that you wrote what one action could you take today to move you toward your purpose? Be courageous. Take that action today.

To download our *7 Days to Get Clarity Series* free visit www.destinystatement.com.

Share your progress! Tweet what most challenged or inspired you from chapter four, The Source Question, to @BeMorExcellent or post it on Barlow Enterprises Facebook page now.

We'll follow you back!

CHAPTER 6

The Gifts Question

Question 4 • What Can I Do?

A man's gift makes room for him, and brings him before great men.

~ King Solomon

Don't Take Your Gifts for Granted

When it comes to fashion, accessories complete and compliment your look by giving you a polished, finished look. As accessories are to your ensemble, car, or home so are your gifts and talents when it comes to fulfilling your destiny. Your gifts compliment and assist you in fulfilling your life's purpose. Gifts are the accessories of life. Your unique gifts give your life and work an unmistakable "bling" and set you apart from the masses.

In the context of living a life of purpose, there are various opinions about what the word gift means. At the Global Destiny Institute, we use the terms gifts and talents interchangeably.

We define gifts and talents as innate abilities that come naturally to you.

Destiny Seed

Gifts are the accessories of life. Your gifts and talents facilitate purposeful living.

Too many people underestimate their gifts or talents. Underestimating your gift especially happens when using your gift is fun or comes easy to you.

Have you taken your gifts for granted? In spite of the fact that we have been teaching people to maximize their gifts for over fifteen years, we understand, because Omar and I have been guilty of it too!

A very successful mentor of mine (Jéneen) had a need. I knew that I could meet the need because I really enjoy research and writing and had written for numerous companies before so I contracted with him to produce an advanced curriculum for a popular training program that he had been teaching internationally for years. He is a speaker, corporate trainer, and network marketing guru so the events, conferences, coaching, e-book development, and other business opportunities that the curriculum affords him further establish and affirm his position as a leading authority in his industry; the curriculum exponentially increases his revenue because it adds additional streams of income to his already thriving enterprises.

The work that I did for his business adds short and long-term value, not only to his business, but to the lives and businesses of those he leads and teaches. To make the deal even sweeter, it was a lot of fun for me to complete the project and my company was paid for doing it. So the question is, why hadn't we been writing curricula for entrepreneurs, executives, speakers, and coaches all along?

Using Your Gifts Creates Win-Win-Win Scenarios

I was in a box. Until someone close to me had a problem that I knew I could solve, I had limited my gift to writing for educational institutions, corporations, and non-profits. Those are the groups for whom I had written curricula and developed programs for years and although there was no reason for me to limit myself, I was just so stuck focusing on the industries that I traditionally served, that I could not see the incredible opportunity for me to help *individuals* with my gift.

Some see the curriculum design process as maddening, but my gifts make it come naturally to me, and doing the work makes me happy. When I recognized that I was guilty of limiting the gift that I had for helping professionals with this service, I created my Custom Cash-Generating Curriculum™ Program. Now that we have expanded the product and services to speakers, coaches, entrepreneurs, and executives, I fulfill my mission on a larger scale.

- **Who said living life on purpose should not spring from acts that bring joy and add value to you and those around you?**
- **Why shouldn't living on purpose come naturally and make you feel fulfilled?**
- **Do you understand that you are limiting your income *and* your happiness by not creating and looking for opportunities where you can be paid exceptionally well for doing what you are gifted to do?**

Eventually, the answers to what to do and how to do it will come to you, but before they do you need quiet yourself.

As you quiet yourself, you will be able to more clearly hear the purposes of your heart speaking to you. As you discipline yourself, you will be positioned to use pillars one and two -- check your heart and dive deep -- from chapter one. Most of all, unique ideas will come to you and you will find ways to use your gifts and talents that produce winning opportunities for you and for everyone in your sphere of influence.

In this chapter, we offer you four essential Destiny Seeds to help you with the gifts question.

Destiny Seeds

Discover what you can do
Perfect your gifts
Love what you perfect
Share what you love

Discover What You Can Do

Allow this fourth question of purpose to challenge you. What can you do? Make a list of answers then ask yourself another question. What else can I do? Interview those who know and love you. Ask them what they think you do well and write it all down in a book that you will always be able to easily access.

Sometimes people who come to us for coaching initially tell us they have no gifts or talents. Others are stuck or frustrated because they have too many gifts and talents and cannot figure out where to focus. Many are skilled at doing things they no longer have a passion for doing, so depending on their particular situation, some partners need help to figure out where to *stop* giving their time and energy.

Of course there are also extremely gifted partners who have yet to recognize the value of their gifts and skills so they have given their gift away, over and over again, for free. We help partners in that situation to represent and assign the proper value to their services so that they can earn income from sharing their gifts.

Everyone has something to give. You have something to give and people are waiting for you to give it. Do not allow the fear of uncertainty to stop you from moving forward. As the sagacious King Solomon affirms, your gifts will make room for you and bring you before great people. Your gifts will propel you into new experiences and possibilities. But in order for this to happen, you have to acknowledge that you are gifted and identify your gifts. You also have to learn how to present your gifts and then be confident and courageous enough to assign the proper value to what you have to offer.

Ultimately, identifying your gifts and talents protects you from becoming, as the saying goes, "A jack of all trades and a master of none." In Mexico, the same phrase goes, "A todo le tiras, y a nada le pegas" which means, "You shoot for everything, but you hit nothing." Be intentional. Think about what you can do. Decide which one to three things you want to do and then really focus on doing those things well. This will prove to be a much better plan than attempting to do everything, and succeeding at doing nothing with excellence.

Encourage [people] to look at themselves and their God-given talents. Success in life revolves around recognizing and using your raw material.

~ Ben Carson

We spoke earlier about how reflecting upon and investigating your childhood is a useful strategy for discovering, or more accurately, for remembering who you are. So is it with discovering your gifts and talents. In *Bone Black: Memories of Girlhood,* best-selling author, literary critic, feminist thinker, mentor and friend of my mind (Jéneen) bell hooks writes,

> *I read poems. I write. That is my destiny [dream] . . . I remember who I am. I am a young poet, a writer. I am here to make words . . . I tell myself stories, write poems, record my dreams. In my journal I write – I belong in this place of words. This is my home. This dark, bone black, inner cave where I am making a world for myself.*

The words are so smartly penned that I can read them again and again. Every single time I read the words I smile. In essence, she says, *"I read . . . I write . . . I am."*

She declares from her youth what she can do and it is from that declaration of what she can do that she decides her future.

Gracie, our little girl, came into this world using her voice to communicate, in no uncertain terms, her expectations, her likes, and her dislikes. From the moment I heard her voice, I knew from the depths of my motherly soul, that I had given life to a dynamic, passionate girl whose voice would be used to unsettle, challenge, and bring change wherever she showed up. Our daughter Grace, Amazing Grace as she named herself when she was three, loves to read, talk, sing, and dance. I barely recall a time when she did not speak complete sentences. Perhaps that is because, since I heard her first cry, she's had such a piercing, demonstrative voice that her wailing sounded like complete sentences to me. From as early as two, Grace would take stacks of books from her shelves, or ours, pile them beside her on the bed or floor and say, "I'm reading, Mommy." Unless she had invited me to read to her, she would cry if I tried to snuggle up next to her to read her a story. It was fine to listen in, but at home and at school, she made it clear, "I am the reader."

In an effort to get her to go to bed, Omar and I would say, "Gracie, you need to read *one* more book and then we will turn off your lights." She was reluctant. She'd negotiate by asking that the books at least remain in her bed, by her side. When the lights were out, all that we could hear is Gracie giggling loudly, crying dramatically (for pretend), or shouting exuberantly as she made up her own, intriguing tales. She was a one woman show. And since she was born, she has been showing us exactly what she can do.

What can you do?

Write down everything that you can do. Don't be modest!

____

____

____

____

____

Perfect Your Gifts

If you wrote more than seems humanly possible to actually do, then this next section is especially for you.

There are Renaissance men and women in our history books, as well as in our midst, and you may be one of them. Nonetheless, even the Renaissance among us have to focus on realizing a few key results at a time. Gifted people, who achieve maximum levels of success, learn quickly that they must exert unfathomable amounts of time, energy, effort, and resources into perfecting their gifts and talents, and into mastering certain skills if they seriously plan to dominate in their fields.

So while gifts and talents are innate abilities that come naturally to you. It is important to note that earning the privilege of being deemed a master at your craft does not come easily.

Which gifts do you love enough to master?

A classic, Hollywood example of paying the price to perfect your gift is dramatically depicted in the Oscar-winning film, *Whiplash*. Despite the fierce debate in some circles about the terribly abusive student-teacher relationship in the movie, our focus here is not on the maniacal instructor, but on the drummer who made the extremely difficult personal decision to make extreme sacrifices to become a master at his craft. He was already gifted to play. That was made clear in the scene that showed us that he was drumming brilliantly as a very young child. But his gift alone would never make him a master. In *Don't Be Scared. BE-speak!*, we talk about the fact that mastery requires you to invest unusual amounts of time, initiative, money, and energy into what comes naturally to you.

Only you can decide how much you are willing to give to perfect your gifts, but you will have to decide. Furthermore, you will need to be ready and willing to consistently make those sacrifices. It's all an unavoidable requirement on the path to greatness. Interestingly, you will be willing to yield to the demands of mastery because while becoming a master at your craft requires what seems like unreasonable sacrifices to others. Love gives. So, whatever your gift is, if you love it enough, you will give what is required for you to advance to the top of your craft.

Here's the secret that liberates all overachieving, multi-talented, people: Just being gifted will never make extraordinary things happen for you. So stop feeling overwhelmed if you can do many things well. The question is simple. What can you do, that you love so much, that you are willing to sacrifice whatever time, initiative, money, and energy necessary to become a master at it?

Destiny Seeds

When it comes to being more excellent in life and in business, being gifted is not enough. Love is not enough. However, the right combination of giftedness, love, and sacrifice will no doubt make you a skillful master who is equipped to make an indelible mark on the world.

Lessons on Mastery From the Masters

In an interview with XXL Magazine from December of 2002, gifted music mogul, producer, and entrepreneur, Jay-Z explains how he sacrifices in the process of perfecting his gift. Jay-Z said:

> *It's all been non-stop man, not looking back and hard work. Hard, hard, hard, work. The good thing about it is it's something I enjoy doing. I expend all of my energy on it. I live here [in the studio]. I live in this studio when I'm making albums. It's all that I do. Like my outside world suffers, everything suffers. I don't see people. I don't go out. I don't hang out much. A friend of mine said she was going to burn her dictionary. She said, 'I'm jealous of words. You love words more than our friendship.'*

Sometimes the people you love most will not be able to understand you at all. They may even complain, dissuade, criticize, and drain your positive energy in various ways. Don't be angry. Expect this. Love them. And move forward. When you decide to Live on Purpose, being misunderstood by those you love most is a part of the plan.

The incredibly brilliant writer and author of *Black Boy,* Richard Wright, explained an experience he had with his classmates when he was in eighth grade. Wright said,

> *My schoolmates could not understand why anyone would want to write a story . . . I knew that I lived in a country in which the aspirations of black people were limited, marked-off. Yet I felt that I had to go somewhere and do something to redeem my being alive . . . In me was shaping a yearning for a kind of consciousness, a mode of being that the way of life about me had said could not be, and upon which the penalty of death had been placed.*

Richard's gift was evident as early as eighth grade and so was his passion for his craft. History makes it clear that Richard Wright perfected his gift. As a matter of fact, Wright became a master at his craft. His book, *Black Boy* became an instant best-seller when it was published in 1945. Wright is an internationally acclaimed writer, the recipient of the Guggenheim Fellowship, author of twenty books and hosts of essays, poems and other writings. The gift he decided to perfect as a child became a gift to the world.

What gift do you have to offer the world? What can you do, that you love so much, that you are willing to sacrifice whatever time, initiative, money, and energy you have to master it? Focus on that gift. Perfect it. Master it. Serve it up with passion and skill. Someone is waiting for you.

Love What You Perfect

George Washington Carver said, "*Anything will give up its secrets if you love it enough.*"

Once you discover what you can do and you decide to invest the time and effort it takes to master your craft, you quickly realize the vital role that love plays in living on purpose. What separates the novice from the master? Essentially, it's what each knows. Because of their love for the gift, masters spend extraordinary amounts of time with their gifts and masters' love of their gifts eventually provoke the craft to give up its secrets. So, masters possess a greater depth of knowledge and understanding of their craft than others do because masters know secrets. The master's adept demonstration of their gift and the awe-inspiring effect that what they do has on the people they serve, prove over and over again the power of perfecting what you love and loving what you perfect.

Consider jazz trumpeter extraordinaire, Mr. Louis Armstrong. Also known as, Pops or Satchmo, Armstrong's love and mastery of his gift caused him to be written into history as one of the most influential jazz artist of all times. In his biography about Louis Armstrong entitled, *An Extravagant Life,* Laurence Bergreen says:

> *Nobody had ever heard anything like it, and his impact cannot be put into words . . . Nor had it ever been heard in Europe, or South America or Africa, but everywhere it would be known as the sound of America. He was not just America's greatest musical performer; he was also a character of epic proportions. For him, music was a heightened form of existence, and he sang and played as if it could never be long enough, or last long enough, or go deep enough, or reach high enough. He believed there could never be enough music in the world.*

It is not easy to ascend to that level, but when you love your gift, you do whatever it takes to masterfully deliver it to the world.

Share What You Love

Love gives. You work to identify and perfect your gifts so that you can share them with the world.

World-renowned surgeon, Dr. Ben Carson said:

> *I truly believe that being a successful neurosurgeon doesn't mean that I'm better than anyone else. It means that I'm fortunate because God gave me the talent to do this job well. I also believe that what talents I have I need to be willing to share with others.*

As a purpose-driven person you have to remember that living in a state of flow not only benefits you, but it benefits every single person and organization with which you connect. It's what you learn and what you give in the process of becoming, that matters most. That is why this fourth component of answering question number four, What can I do? is so important.

For what cause or for whom are you willing to sacrifice so much? Why are you willing to perfect your gift to that degree for this?

Let's review and learn from the true stories of how sharing your gift can totally transform your life.

Destiny Seeker #1:

Oprah: A Classic Case Study in the Power of Sharing Your Gift

Oprah Winfrey is a cultural icon. Masses of people listen for what Oprah says. Many at least give her commentary some thought. Her popularity transcends class, gender, status, and race.

An endorsement by Ms. Oprah Winfrey will certainly put you on the fast track to notoriety. Just ask the many authors, counselors, singers, and others whose careers experienced quantum leaps after connecting with her.

For twenty-five years, Oprah dazzled audiences with her signature interviews, and who can forget the fact that she has given away millions of dollars both on and off the air.

In principle, Oprah is just talking. She sits with people and has a conversation. Yet her ability to talk has made her a billionaire. Oprah uses her gift, which she has obviously mastered, and in doing so, she dominates in her industry and inspires the world.

When you know Oprah's story, you find that she has always been fond of talking. Oprah has always had linguistic and interpersonal gifts. At the age of three, Oprah was precocious and bookish. Her lifelong love for books gives us further insight as to why the internationally beloved *Oprah's Book Club* began. *Oprah's Book Club* is her childhood passion on steroids!

After winning the Miss Black Tennessee contest in college, Oprah sought a career in broadcasting. Extremely gifted, Oprah was hired as a reporter while she was still a student at Tennessee State University. By 1976 she was working in Baltimore for ABC-TV. Unfortunately, Oprah began to have trouble at the television station. When interviewing people, she visibly expressed her empathy and compassion for victims. This reaction was unheard of for a newscaster but she admits to having to often fight back tears during her interviews. On one occasion, she was threatened with a dismissal because she refused to interview a distraught woman who had just survived a raging fire that had taken the lives of several young children. Oprah felt that to interview the woman at that time was an unnecessary intrusion on her grief. Nonetheless, she eventually, yet hesitantly, complied with the station manager and conducted the interview. Later however, Oprah apologized to the family during a live broadcast.

Following this incident, Oprah's manager moved her to the morning talk-show. Although viewed as a demotion, Oprah exclaimed, "This is what I was born to do. It feels like breathing to me!"

Within five months the show became the third highest rated show in syndication. Shortly afterwards, Oprah was offered the host slot on WLS-TV's A.M. Chicago show. That was 1984. The rest is history.

Think about it. As soon as Oprah began hosting the morning show, she felt like she was doing what she was born to do. It was hard work and yet it was as natural as breathing. She was using her gift of talking combined with her gift of compassion and her journalistic skills. Instead of allowing her station manager's advice to change her format and her style, Oprah found work in an environment that would celebrate her gift. Her choice to identify, perfect and share the gifts she loved made the multi-billion dollar difference in her life and in the lives of people around the world.

Destiny Seeker #2

Steven Spielberg: A Classic Case Study in the Power of Sharing Your Gift

Oprah Winfrey's story clearly demonstrates how identifying what you love to do, mastering it, and perfecting it can positively impact your life and the lives of the people you are destined to help and inspire.

Let's examine the story of another wildly famous Destiny Seeker, Steven Spielberg. Spielberg was born in Cincinnati, Ohio in 1946. From the age of twelve, Spielberg knew that he wanted to be a movie director. When he was seventeen, a tour he took of Universal Studios changed his life forever. Excited about finally being at the studio, Spielberg took off from the guided tour to watch the filming of a real movie and he ended up meeting the head of the editorial department.

Knowing that he wanted an opportunity to share his gift and skill of film-making on a large scale, Spielberg put on a suit, stuffed his father's briefcase with a sandwich and two candy bars and returned to Universal Studios. He strolled confidently past the guards, into the lot, and affixed the title, "Steven Spielberg Director" to an abandoned trailer he had found. He spent the remainder of the summer meeting directors, writers, and editors as an intern and guest of Universal Studios. This was young Spielberg's dream.

In 1968, he made his first short film. It was a twenty-six minute production entitled *Amblin.* The then Vice President of Production for the television unit of Universal Studios saw his work and offered Spielberg a long-term deal with the studio. This made him the youngest director who ever signed with a major Hollywood studio for a long-term deal.

When you think of his amazing body of work -- E.T., Back to the Future, Gremlins, Goonies, Indiana Jones and the Last Crusade, Jurassic Park, Schindler's List, Saving Private Ryan, The Color Purple, Amistad, and others -- remember that Spielberg realized that he had talent and he took the risk, at seventeen-years old, to immerse himself into the industry that he loved and into a craft that he was committed to mastering. Look what an impact his tenacity made on his life and on the millions of us around the world who have enjoyed and been inspired by his films.

Destiny Seeker #3

J.K. Rowlings: A Classic Case Study in the Power of Sharing Your Gift

Surely the stories of Oprah and Steven Spielberg are convincing examples of how important it is to identify and master the use of your gift if you want to live on purpose. Nonetheless, if only for the sake of telling another awe-inspiring story, let's see what we can learn from the life of author J.K. Rowlings.

Rowlings sold over 450 million Harry Potter books and millions more of the other titles she has authored. When asked, "When did you first want to be a writer?" she responded,

> *Always . . . as soon as I knew what writers were, I wanted to be one. I've got the perfect temperament for a writer; perfectly happy alone in a room, making things up.*

Rowlings says that she had been writing continuously since the age of six. In fact, during her childhood, Rowlings shares that she was known for telling a tremendous number of stories. Sometimes, she would sit on her sister, Di's, back to make her listen to the stories and at other times they turned the stories into games in which J.K and Di acted out the characters.

Like Oprah and Spielberg, it is clear that J.K. had a special gift from an early age, and like Oprah and Spielberg, J.K. Rowlings was willing to go to great lengths to exercise her gift. J.K. raised her young daughter and worked as a teacher while also working to get her first book published. Her schedule was nearly impossible to keep but she was possessed by the idea of Harry Potter, so she kept writing. All the while she was thinking, "Unless I finish this book soon, I may never get it finished!"

J.K. Rowlings' decision to finish what she started dramatically transformed her life and her legacy. It is a powerful example that astounding things happen when you use your gift and relentlessly pursue your vision. Rowlings eventually got her book published. Interestingly enough, Rowlings never thought that the world would respond so incredibly favorably to this figment of her imagination named "Harry Potter." But the world did. As a result, a little girl who had a lifelong love affair with stories became an internationally acclaimed writer and multi-billionaire.

The Most Sensational Seed of All

When you share your gift, you unleash unimaginable favor in your life. In the process of perfecting and sharing your gift there may be times that you feel exhausted, misunderstood, or ashamed. There may be times that you contemplate abandoning your gifts and talents to do something easier. Don't. It is critical that you finish what you started. It is critical that you share what you have with others.

Have you ever eaten or heard of Famous Amos cookies? Do you know what made Famous Amos Famous? Fame found Wally Amos because he was sharing his gift of baking cookies simply to say thank you to his friends, but people loved his cookies so much that they started placing orders! Eventually, Wally ended up with so many orders that he had to start a company to meet the demand for his cookies.

What began as a seed -- a small way of saying thank you by sharing his gift-- grew into an incredibly successful enterprise.

Using Your Gift Requires a Mental Shift

Imagine who will respond when you start to share your gift? Imagine who will be affected because you dare to share what you love with the world?

> *When you love what you do, work is play.*
>
> *~ Mark Twain*

Sometimes we associate work with drudgery and it becomes very difficult to imagine getting paid to play, but this is exactly the mental shift that you have to make when you decide to use your gifts to live on purpose. Proper use of your skillfully honed gifts will always position you to create wealth.

In the ancient parable of the talents, Jesus tells how three servants are given goods by their master. One servant receives five talents, another two, and another one. The first servant who received five talents traded and made five other talents; the second servant who received two talents traded and made two others. On the contrary, the one that received one talent buried his talent. According to the parable, the master returned to see what his servants had done. To the two servants who had increased their share, the master said, "Well done, good and faithful servants: you have been faithful over a few things, I will make you ruler over many things." The master called the servant who buried his talent wicked and lazy. Then, the master took what that servant had and gave his talent to the servant who had the most.

Don't Be Scared. Live on Purpose!

> *We deny our talents and abilities because to acknowledge or to confess them ... would commit us to use them.*
>
> *~Earl Loomis*

Perhaps the servant who buried his talent thought that what he had to share was insignificant in light of what the others possessed. It is easy, when you look at those around you, to feel like what you have is not enough. Comparing causes you to focus on what you don't have, highlights your weaknesses, and causes you to underestimate the sacrifices that others have made to acquire what they have. This is exactly why it is unwise to compare yourself with others.

As we discussed in chapter two, people of purpose don't waste time comparing themselves with others, instead they always ask the better questions. In this case, the only question that matters is, "What's in your hand?" Regardless of how much or how little you have, when you ask yourself the right questions, fear gives way to endless possibilities.

No Excuses Please

The master did not expect every servant to perform in the same way. That was not the measure of success. But the master did expect all of the servants to do something with what they had been given.

Three talent-squandering culprits are laziness, procrastination, and fear. Both prevent from cultivating what we have. Your greatest opportunities are always disguised as work. Faithfulness over what seems like a little always sets you up to rule over so much more. In fact, the servant with five talents exemplifies for us how the Law of Attraction works. As a result of developing his talents, he received the talent from the one who buried his.

When you are intentional about working *on* and *with* what you have, you will invariably produce more and more will be given to you. You will become a magnet for success.

The BE Challenge

From which case study did you learn the most? Write one to three lessons that most impacted you. Explain why you chose those lessons.

____

____

____

____

____

____

We love hearing from you. Share your progress! Tweet the Destiny Seeds from chapter six, The Gifts Question, to @BeMorExcellent or post it on Barlow Enterprises Facebook page now.

We'll follow you back!

CHAPTER 7

The Vision Question

Question 5 • Where am I going?

Visionary statements and actions come from a completely different place in the human psyche from predictions, forecasts, scenarios, or cynical, downer assertions of political impossibility. They come from commitment, responsibility, confidence, values, longing, love, treasured dreams, our innate sense of what is right and good. A vision articulates a future that someone deeply wants, and does it so clearly and compellingly that it summons up the energy, agreement, sympathy, political will, creativity, resources, or whatever to make that future happen.

~ Donella H. Meadows

The natural progression of living on purpose gives birth to your personal vision. Vision is the product of purpose. While purpose addresses the "*Why*" of your life, your vision captures "*Where*" your purpose will take you. Properly defined, vision is a clear portrait of conditions that do not currently exist; it is the capacity to see things as they could be.

All high-achieving men and women are visionaries. In fact, when we think about "what makes the great great," many would agree that vision – *the capacity to see things as they could be* – is certainly at the top of the list.

Experts suggest that one of the most important things you can do is to develop a vision for your life. After thirty-three hundred studies of leadership, researchers have concluded, that there was one quality that all leaders all seemed to have in common, and that was the quality of vision.

I (Omar) used to give my students at North Penn an assignment to interview several adults over fifty years old. They asked the people they interviewed, "What would you do differently if you could start your life over again?"

The last time I gave that assignment, 1500 people over the age of 50 were interviewed and the majority of respondents said that they would have gotten more education. I learned something interesting from the results of that assignment. I learned that pursuing education was not the real issue. The issue was that many of those interviewed did not, at the point in their lives where they made the decision not to further their education, see education as a priority because they were unclear of what they wanted to accomplish in life. They respond that they would have gotten more education because, in hindsight, they realize that they could have achieved more if they had learned more.

Carter G. Woodson pinpointed the phenomenon perfectly when he said:

> *When you control a man's thinking you do not have to worry about his actions. You do not have to tell him to stand here or go yonder. He will find his 'proper place' and will stay in it. You do not need to send him to the back door. He will go without being told. In fact, if there is no back door, he will cut one for his special benefit. His education makes it necessary.*

Acquiring formal schooling is not the issue. We already made it clear that schooling and education are two different things. The point is that any institution, and we are all part of several institutions, that does not require people to know about and use what they know about themselves, to make their lives, or the lives of those the institutions serves better, minimizes its chances to be effective because it cripples its ability to truly activate and thereby benefit from the potential of the people with whom it interacts. Therein lies the problem.

Destiny Seed

Living on Purpose and without fear always demands that you commit to lifelong learning.

However, as evidenced by the many successful individuals who dropped out of top-tier schools to pursue their dream, sometimes traditional, formal schooling can hinder those who truly know what they are passionate about doing in life. What the interviews by my former students reveal is that when you do not know your reason for being, what you think about or imagine for your future is likely to be so small that you will forego opportunities that would have positioned you to create your best life.

The Resurrection Power of Vision

Where there no vision, the people perish.

- King Solomon

Vision has resurrection power! Vision provides hope. Vision protects your focus and promotes self-discipline. Your vision for your life influences your character, your life's work and what you study, your friends, your attitude towards life, your service to others, and even your diet.

Before construction begins on new structures, a sign is posted that says, "Coming Soon." Despite the fact that the site is often vacant or in disarray, the "Coming Soon" sign provides onlookers with a vision of what's to come. When the building is finally finished, we're fascinated, but those responsible for the construction are not amazed. Because of their plans, their vision was clear. They already knew what the final product would look like. You must do the same. Make the time to plan your future and then post a "Coming Soon" sign for your life. Your Destiny Statement™ is your blueprint.

We all have stories of rising from desperate looking situations. When we tell the story of Victor Frankl, the silence in the room is deafening. We have told his story hundreds of times to thousands of listeners. It is truly a story of how *lux in tenebris lucet,* which in Latin is translated, *how light shines in the darkness.*

Few people have had to rise from such horrific and intense suffering.

Dr. Victor Frankl survived the Jewish Holocaust. He writes about the suffering that many Jews endured within these camps. Stripped of his identity, Frankl became number 119,104. Every day he watched his fellow prisoners fight for food, suffer through the agony of starvation and sleeplessness, and endure savage beatings. He was always fearful, hoping and praying that he would not be called to stand in line for the gas chamber or the crematorium.

Due to his training as a psychologist, Frankl noticed something profound among the sufferers. In spite of the mental and physical torment, the spiritual life of the prisoners deepened. They were able to "retreat from their terrible surroundings to a life of inner riches and spiritual freedom."

> *One day, while marching in a work line, one man said to Frankl, "I wonder what our wives would say if they could see us now!" Despite the frostbite, the hunger, the excruciating pain, and the fact that Frankl had no clue whether his wife was dead or alive, he suddenly captured a vision of his wife. It was typical for the captives to be*

> *separated from their families, yet, in Frankl's vision, he heard his wife answering him. He saw her smile and he saw her encouraging look which to him, 'was more luminous than the sun which was beginning to rise.'*

Then, he had a revelation. For the first time in his life he realized that:

> *Love is the ultimate and the highest goal to which man can aspire. Then I grasped the meaning of the greatest secret that human poetry and human thought and belief have to impart: the salvation of man is through love and in love. I understood how a man who has nothing left in this world still may know bliss, be it only for a brief moment, in the contemplation of his beloved. In a position of utter desolation, when man cannot express himself in positive action, when his only achievement may consist in en during his sufferings in the right way – an honorable way – in such a position man can, through loving contemplation of the image he carries of his beloved, achieve fulfillment.*

In this instance, the vision of Frankl's beloved wife kept him alive, but here's the principle. When you find something you love and capture a detailed, emotionalized vision of it, you can endure. Your vision overrides the hardships of your present and your past and gives you hope for a bright future.

Frankl survived the Holocaust and eventually gained international renown. He showed people that many Holocaust survivors refused to commit suicide because, even in the midst of unthinkable suffering, they managed to find the purpose of their lives. Frankl's vision of his beloved wife was so vivid that he says that he asked her questions, and she answered; she questioned, and he answered back. Imagine the power that your vision for your life has.

Do not be afraid of what you may lose or of what others will think or say about you. Allow yourself to be consumed and revived by the vision you create for your life.

Future Orientation

Once you surrender to the vision you create for your life, you have to adopt a long term perspective or strong future orientation. The term is popularly used as a financial and economic term, and as a psychological and educational term. In both instances, the phrase describes the propensity of a culture, agent or individual to delay gratification in the interest of greater rewards and benefits at some time in the future.

In the late 1950s and early 1960s, Dr. Edward Banfield of Harvard University studied many of the factors that contribute to individual financial success over a person's lifetime. Banfield's insights are also important for understanding the principles of vision. Banfield concludes that "time perspective" takes precedence over all other factors.

Banfield realized that people at the highest social and economic levels make decisions and sacrifices that may not pay off for many years, sometimes not even in their own lifetimes. In many respects, these individuals "plant trees under which they will never sit." People with long term perspective, or strong future orientations, think more about what the consequences of their actions might be.

On the other hand, people at the lowest levels of society were found to have short term perspectives. Research indicates that these groups focus primarily on immediate gratification and that they are more likely to engage in behaviors that will have negative consequences in the long term. Banfield claims that this preoccupation with instant gratification prohibits them from paying the price for long term benefits.

As with any findings, one could debate why these were the results of his study.

Unfortunately, developing a long-term perspective is a discipline that many disenfranchised people may not develop and that is understandable when just meeting life's basic necessities is a struggle.

The goal here, however, is to show that research affirms that becoming a more future-focused thinker better positions us to enjoy the benefits associated with clarifying our vision. This is why Texas oil billionaire Bunker Hunt stated that:

> *First you must decide what you want specifically; and second, you must decide that you are willing to pay the price to make it happen – and then pay the price. If you don't take that second step, you'll never have what you want in the long-term.*

Be Prepared to Fight the Tension

Author Robert Fritz explains a process called "Sustaining Structural Tension" in relationship to vision. Fritz says that the mind ultimately has one desire and that is to see only one image at a time. Consequently, the mind goes into overdrive trying to integrate "what is" and "what could be." People who focus on "what is" will create more of "what is." People who focus on "what could be" will begin to create what could be. Without doubt, the tension in this process can be difficult to manage. It is easier to focus on what is.

Nonetheless, if you persist through the tension you will no longer "live out" what is but you will outpace reality and transition into the vision you want to become your reality.

<u>Destiny Seed</u>

Visualization will eventually bring realization but you have to be willing to decide what you want, pay the price, and then remain focused on your future until you show up there!

Vision Produces People Who Take Action

Vision is the best manifestation of creative imagination and the primary motivation of human action. It is the ability to see beyond our present reality, to create, to invent what does not yet exist, to become what we not yet are. It gives us the capacity to live out our imagination instead of our memory.

The late, brilliant, businessman, speaker and author of the *Seven Habits for Highly Effective People,* Stephen Covey, reminds us in that quote to focus on moving towards our imaginations for ourselves so that we can escape slipping into memories past. In essence, when you focus on imagining you automatically begin to move towards your vision and away from your past.

Vision forces you to perpetually take action.

In 2007, Jéneen's father passed away unexpectedly. Her father left us something especially valuable. In her father's office, we discovered James Allen's classic book *As a Man Thinketh,* originally published in 1902. One of the most fascinating stories told by Allen is a story of an unschooled, impoverished boy working a dead-end job.

Despite the boy's condition, he dreams of better things. He envisions a life of grace, beauty, refinement, and intelligence. To achieve this life the boy mentally builds up this vision and pretty soon the vision begins to possess him. He begins to *take action*, and he utilizes all of his spare time and resources to develop his powers and talents. Very soon, due to the alteration of his mind, his circumstances, his environment, and his relationships can no longer hold him. They are out of harmony with his mentality. Allen notes that years later this young man holds world-wide influence and power. Many will ask, "How did this happen?" The answer is that the once impoverished boy developed a vision for his life. You must do the same.

May the words of James Allen inspire you to take action:

> *The vision that you glorify in your mind, the ideal that you enthrone in your heart – this you will build your life by, this you will become.*

Let's take action now by writing what you imagine for your future.

Imagine a wonderful celebration where friends, loved ones, and associates from all walks of life have come to honor you. Imagine this joyous occasion in as much detail as you possibly can. Describe the place, the people, the food, the decorations and everything else that comes to mind. See these individuals in your mind's eye as they stand, one by one, to pay tribute to you. Assume that you have lived your life on purpose. You have maximized your potential.

What are these people saying about you?

____

____

____

____

____

What characteristics are you most remembered for?

____

____

____

____

____

What outstanding contributions are they mentioning?

____

____

____

____

____

What important differences have you made in their lives?

____
____
____
____
____

Beware the Naysayers!

Once you begin to clarify and pursue your vision for your life, your true friends and your enemies will wake up! In other words, you don't really know who your true friends and enemies are until you start to fulfill your vision.

By beginning to think about and answer the question, *Where am I going?* you give the people in your spheres of influence the opportunity to respond to who you are becoming and what you intend to do. On one hand, starting to answer the question will attract new, supportive, equally ambitious friends and colleagues. On the other hand, a number of people will be offended that you have decided to boldly pursue your dreams. You *will* start to outgrow some relationships. Prepare for the backlash! You may hear, "Oh, you've changed!" "Who do you think you are?" "You think you are better than we are, don't you?"

Never fear. You may have to walk alone until you find people who can understand, nurture, and celebrate your vision.

In the meantime, in the words of our mentor and friend Mr. Stephen McKiernan, "Carry on!"

BE Challenge

Tweet your biggest take away from chapter seven, The Vision Question, to @BeMorExcellent or post it on Barlow Enterprises Facebook page now.

We'll follow you back!

CHAPTER 8

Destiny Statement ™ Development: Phase I

How to Add Time to Your Life

My mother (Jéneen) used to say, "Chile, don't go putting the cart before the horse." She knew that I was ambitious and feisty. She knew that I liked to work fast. But in her quiet way, she'd wisely remind me that there is a set time and order to everything. My mother knew that for things to go well, I had to slow down and make as much time to reflect upon why I wanted to take certain paths, as I was willing to invest in working to achieve my goals.

Sometimes we are so caught up in the whirlwind of things that we have to do, people to help, projects to finish, and places to go, that when we stop to reflect on how we have used our time, we end up horrified to find that more than half of the things we did were not very important to us at all. Life is too short to live unintentionally.

To avoid wasting our time (our life), Destiny Seekers pause often. We reflect, write, and take action on the big questions of life that we have reviewed throughout this book. We check to make sure that we are activating the *The Four Pillars of Purpose* in our lives. This is how we flow through life. This is how we avoid getting tripped up from running so fast that we never realize that the proverbial cart and horse are all mixed up and that they are not moving at all.

While it takes time and patience to achieve what is written on your Destiny Statement,™ we have found that, on average, it takes about eight hours to finish all five components of the Destiny Statement™. One of our favorite things about the process is that writing and thinking in this way gives you the clarity and the confidence to know what to say "yes" to and, most importantly of all, having your personal mission and vision statements help you to identify those opportunities to which you need to unapologetically say "no thank you."

What is a Destiny Statement?

As one of our Executive Partners, Timothy said to us, The Destiny Statement™ is your "blueprint for living a life of passion and purpose." It is a working document that serves as your guide to living on purpose.

The statement consists of five elements: your custom mission statement, your mission-aligned vision statement (written in the seven key areas of life), your predominant intelligences, your strengths, and your destiny-driven deadlines.

What is a Personal Mission Statement?

A personal mission statement is your written reason for being. In no more than one sentence, your personal mission statement clearly and concisely states three things: your impact, your ethics, and your people. In the Global Destiny Institute, we call this impact, ethics, people mix your IEP Formula.

What is a Personal Vision Statement?

A personal vision statement is your written vision for yourself in all seven key areas of life. In the Global Destiny Institute, we do not teach people to work to achieve balance. We believe that the pursuit of living a life in balance, where balance is defined as everything being equal or even, can be as maddening and unattainable as trying to be perfect. Perfection is a myth and so is living a balanced life.

On the contrary, to be aware that there are multiple dimensions, or as we call them, key areas of life, and to articulate what you envision for yourself in all of those areas is exhilarating and productive. The goal is to be aware of all seven areas, to have a clear vision for your life in all seven areas, and to identify, based upon your mission and the stage of life you are in, what percentage of your time should be designated to each of the key areas based on what you need in your life at that time.

We encourage you to try to attain *synergy* among the areas and to be at peace with the fact that not all of the areas will be everything that you envision all at once.

In your Destiny Statement™, your vision statement is written after your personal mission statement and it consists of at least one paragraph for all seven key areas of life.

We guide you through all seven key areas of life, and all of the vital steps for exactly how to write your vision statement, in our Executive Programs.

Mission and Vision Are Not The Same

Mission and vision are not synonymous. Your mission is the big picture statement for your life. It is your written reason for existence that should be memorized and can be stated in one sentence. Your mission is a snapshot of **why** you are here. Your vision, on the other hand, explains in detail **how** you *see* yourself working on the why of your life.

Writing Your Personal Mission Statement

Writing your personal mission statement is the first phase of the process. In phase one of the Destiny Statement™ process, writing the actual personal mission statement, we teach you to use a method we call the IEP Formula which stands for Impact, Ethics, and People.

You will write your personal mission statement in three distinct sections. Think of it like building an ice-cream sundae with your favorite ice cream, whipped cream, and a cherry on top. Whether you want to build your dessert in a cone, a cup, or inside of your favorite crystal dish, the foundation on which your Destiny Statement™ is built are: *The Four Pillars of Purpose* and all five of the big questions of life that we covered in this book.

Your statement may appear to be just a piece of paper, but it is so much more. People we helped write Destiny Statements™ as far back as fifteen years ago send us testimonials on how their mission and vision are still inspiring, guiding, transforming, and coming to fruition in their lives!

Just writing a statement is better than not having anything, but the statement by itself does not change your life or your business. Understanding the philosophy and the basis of living on purpose is what matters. When you know why you are writing your Destiny Statement™ the document becomes a powerful and enduring force in your life.

One of the most powerful examples of how deeply and positively the Destiny Statement™ process impacts people's lives was shared with us a few years ago when a gentlemen called our office and said, "Is this still Barlow Enterprises." I'd answered his call that day. I (Jéneen) said, "Yes, this is Barlow Enterprises. How may I help you?" The man went on to explain that several years earlier he had attended a professional development seminar that we had conducted at The United Way. I was delighted that he had called. "I am holding my personal mission statement in my hand," he excitedly said to me. "Your process made such a difference in my life that I want you to help my daughter. Her birthday is coming soon so I need to help her to complete her Destiny Statement™ before for her sweet-sixteen."

Impacting generations with the critical message of living life on purpose -- *that* is why we do what we do!

Mission Statement Part One: IMPACT

Genuinely living on purpose results from strategic, inspired service to the people you were destined to impact with your energy, your example, and your words. As Maya said,

> *I've learned that people will forget what you said, people will forget what you did, but people will never forget how you made them feel.*

When you think about how you want to make people feel during their time with you, what words come to mind?

After people experience your work, your presentation, or some interaction with you, if they were asked to complete the following thought, what words do you want them to use to describe how you impacted them?

To access our comprehensive IMPACT Word Bank, download the free *Destiny Statement™ Phase I: Guide to Writing Your Personal Mission Statement Usingthe3-Step IEP Formula* visit:

www.destinystatement.com.

*Quickly brainstorm. Write all of the words that describe the impact that you want your presence and your work to have on the people you meet.

It does not matter what state you are in now. Imagine. All things being ideal, how do you impact the lives of others?

Set your timer to ten minutes. Start writing now.

____

____

____

____

____

***Access our comprehensive IMPACT Word Bank online to help you.**

All of the words that you wrote or circled are important to you, but let's push to be as clear as possible by choosing just one, two, or three (but no more than three) of the impact words you chose.

Look again at the words you chose. Read all of the words aloud. Be sensitive to how you feel when you hear those impact words and circle only the words that *most* affect you when you hear them. Now use the one, two, or three words that you circled to complete the sentence below.

I was just with ______________________________ and now I feel/I feel like I can,

(insert your name here)

____________________, ____________________, and

insert impact word #1 *insert impact word #2*

____________________.

insert impact word #3

Mission Statement Part Two: ETHICS

Now that you have selected the one to three impact words that best describe how you want people to feel after they have interacted with you, let's complete the second step in building your personal mission statement.

How do you decide what is good or correct? Everything that you do and say, as well as, what you choose not to do or say, are products of your philosophy on what's good and what's bad or on what is ethical.

You want people to feel a certain way after they have left you because you highly regard a certain set of guiding beliefs and ideals. These beliefs and ideals are based on what you have come to believe is ethical and, ultimately, your ethics shape your ethos or your character.

To download the free *Destiny Statement™ Phase I: Guide to Writing Your Personal Mission Statement Using the 3-Step IEP Formula* visit: www.destinystatement.com.

*Quickly brainstorm. Write all of the character traits that you possess now or that you want to develop.

It does not matter what state you are in now. Imagine. All things being ideal, which character traits do you want people to mention when they think of you and the ethics with which you operate?

Set your timer to ten minutes. Start writing now.

____

____

____

____

____

***Access our comprehensive ETHICS Word Bank online to help you.**

All of the words that you wrote or circled in the guide are important to you, but let's push to be as clear as possible by choosing just one, two, or three (but no more than three) of the words you chose. Look again at the words your list. Read all of the words aloud. Be sensitive to how you feel when you hear each character trait. Circle the traits that *most* affect you when you hear them. Now use the one, two, or three words that you circled to complete the sentence below.

I hold these three character traits in the highest regard. Consequently, I will conduct myself in ways that cause these traits to be associated with my work and my name:

____________________, ____________________, ____________________

character trait #1 *character trait #2* *character trait #3*

Mission Statement Part Three: PEOPLE

Let's finish your personal mission statement with the most important detail of all. Who are you here to serve? Too many people are content with saying things like, "I am a people-person," or " I just really want to help people." These are not sufficient replies when asked what you want to do with your life. People who are seriously living on purpose are specific about why they are here, about how they see themselves fulfilling that why, *and* about whom they are here to serve.

Destiny Seekers are not vague. Time is too short for ambiguity. There is no time to be afraid of being specific. Sometimes people are afraid to be specific because they feel that they will leave some group out. The reality is that until you focus and dominate in at least one area of expertise, with a specific group of people, you will not be equipped to expand your influence.

In our experience as national speakers, educators, and coaches: *Those dead set on doing everything for everyone, usually only succeed at not doing much of anything for anyone.* You will not limit yourself by choosing. On the contrary, you actually increase your likelihood of expanding your influence when you state your people groups with confidence.

Stop Being Afraid To Be Specific.

Living on Purpose is about service. Specifically who are you here to serve? You have to decide and then start working strategically to reach that *specific group(s) of people*.

The people you want to serve will be found in two distinct places, so this final, people-group defining step in the personal mission statement building process is divided into two sections: Industries and Causes.

In what industries or causes do you need to be active, in order to most benefit the people you want to help?

Go back to the questions of purpose in chapter five. How did you answer the question about what hurts you? Who do you cry most for when you see them in need? Do you see a common theme when it comes to the people you loved to work with? What kind of work do you enjoy doing so much that you would do that work for free?

To download the free *Destiny Statement™ Phase I: Guide to Writing Your Personal Mission Statement Using the 3-Step IEP Formula* visit: www.destinystatement.com.

*Quickly brainstorm. Write all of the industries or causes you need to be associated with or circle them on the lists in the guide.

It does not matter what field of work you are in now. Maybe you need to pursue a new path. Maybe you are on the right path. Either way, if everything was is ideal, to which industries and causes would you give your time, expertise, money and energy?

Set your timer to ten minutes. Start writing now.

____

____

Access our comprehensive PEOPLE Word Bank at www.destinystatement.com to help you.

All of the words that you wrote are important, but let's push to be as clear as possible by choosing just one, two, or three (but no more than three) of the industries or causes you listed above. Look again at the industries and causes you chose. Read all of them aloud. Be sensitive to how you feel when you hear each of them. Circle the people-groups that *most* affect or intrigue you when you hear them. Now use the one, two, or three industries or causes that you circled or listed above to complete this sentence:

I am most interested in reaching people served by the following industries or causes:

________________________, ________________________, and

industry cause #1 *industry cause #2*

________________________.

industry cause #3

Mission Statement Grand Finale
PUTTING IT ALL TOGETHER

My mission is to:
(insert your 3 impact words)

______________________, ______________________, and

____

for
(insert your 3 ethics words)

______________________, ______________________, and

____

while demonstrating the characteristics of
(insert your 3 causes/people groups)

______________________, ______________________, and

____

Congratulations!

You completed Phase I of the Destiny Statement™ process. Now you have an in-depth understanding of the foundations of how to ***Live on Purpose*** and you have your very own . . .

CUSTOM PERSONAL MISSION STATEMENT!

A Heartfelt Letter To You From Omar & Jéneen

Dear Destiny Seeker,

Life is precious. Every now and then we are reminded of how precious life is. In 2007, my friend, Michael White, died tragically. There are few days that go by that I don't think about Mike. We were childhood friends. We shared skateboards, football games, car rides, bikes, food, clothes, and plenty of laughs and good times. We were so close that I recall sharing Burger King's birthday crowns with this guy. For almost twenty years he performed a sacred act for me, an act that all of the males in my community deem sacred. He cut my hair! Yet my barber, my friend, was snatched away in an instant.

To compound the loss, in the process of researching and writing for this book, my father, Robert Barlow, transitioned on to what he would call, "Glory!" That was the spring of 2012. (Omar)

Life is precious. The gregarious laughter and succulent aromas and tastes my family shared on Thanksgiving of 2007 turned, within five days, into a nightmare. My father, Thomas Arthur Winters, suddenly and mysteriously fell ill. We are not certain exactly what caused him to become so sick, so suddenly, but within thirteen days of being rushed to the emergency room, my dad was dead.

That year and early the next year, were times of great loss. My precious baby niece, Lydia Winters; and my life-long sister-friend Kimara (Kimmy) Garrison were both snatched away in 2007. January 2008, brought the passing of my extraordinary, internationally acclaimed, champion bodybuilding aunt, Marjorie Newlin.

Suddenly, in 2011, four short years later, just as I was beginning to catch my breath from the whirlwind of the 2007 losses, a routine emergency room visit unfolded into a cancer diagnosis. Nine months later Sondra Elizabeth Winters, my mother and dearest friend of all, was dead. (Jéneen)

It seems surreal, but in April of 2014, shortly after the release of my first book, *Don't Be Scared. BEspeak!,* I learned that I needed to have surgery for a mass that was found in my body. Statistics indicate that fewer than five in one million people in America, who have this rare mass, ever find the source of the problem. I consider it a miracle that I did. After quickly working through a lot of information, traveling for various opinions, and of course much prayer and support from our family and friends, I (Jéneen) survived a seven hour, life-saving surgery.

Life is precious.

If we are graced to live long enough, life grants us all stories of pain and loss. Instead of asking, "Why is this happening to us?" We have learned, even under the weight of tremendous pain, to ask "What is the lesson? What are we to learn? How are we to change, to give, and to grow?"

Now, more than ever, we embrace the importance of love, purposeful, fun-filled, healthy living, and time well-spent with those you love.

I (Omar) have been teaching the same message for nearly fifteen years. Yet, it was in the face of the sudden deaths of people who I loved that I became more committed to my life's work of answering and helping others to answer two questions:

1. **For what purpose were you born?**
2. **How will you fulfill that purpose?**

There are three activists-scholars whom I (Jéneen) admire and whom I consider my mentors. In grieving the losses of my father, my mother, family and friends the work and words of bell hooks, Dr. Cornell West, and Muhammad Yunus comfort and challenge me. Their messages and examples of defying the odds, challenging norms, embracing sustained solitude and reflection, living and loving out loud, and service to the least of these keep inspiring and moving me from deep darkness into my destiny. I have been committed to creating and teaching since my first stroke upon a canvas at age nine and since my first oratorical contest over fifteen years ago. Yet, in the face of what I call "heart-wrenching suddenlies," I too became more committed to my life's work of challenging myself and walking with others in answering the questions of:

- **What are you to discover in solitude?**
- **How are you to speak truth to power?**
- **Why are you afraid?**

Once we commit to discover and fulfill our life's work, we embark upon lives rich with meaning and service. We consistently escape, even if narrowly, the potentially paralyzing sadness and fear which reach for us throughout our lives. Instead, we begin to use our life's most valuable gift – time -- with the utmost wisdom and care.

Essentially, we have written this book for three distinct reasons: to equip you to *think about,* to *write about,* and to *take action* on your passion in ways that move you towards remembering your dreams, realizing your dreams, and making your dreams come true. We seek not just to inspire and motivate you but to educate you.

To paraphrase the extraordinary philosopher of business, the late Jim Rohn, motivation speeds us up, but education turns us around!

You have read this book and thoughtfully completed the exercises. You have written the first part of your Destiny Statement™ -- your personal mission statement – but you will also have become a student of one of life's most important, most neglected topics of study – YOU.

Information about you is the most essential information that you gather as you work through this book.

DON'T BE SCARED. LIVE ON PURPOSE! guides you through the strategic thinking, planning, and research required to prepare you to Live Your More Excellent Life. If you thoughtfully completed and followed-through with the exercises, you are destined to enjoy the success that comes from activating what we call the Promise of Penned Possibilities. The promise, paraphrased, claims:

Write your vision, taking care to write it so plainly that those that read it can run with the possibilities that the written vision holds. Be patient and remember that the vision will only become manifest at an appointed time, but at the end of that time rest assured that your vision will speak truth and life to you and to the lives of many who you may never know. It will take time to see your dreams come true, but wait for it; because what you desire is sure to come to you.

Destiny is defined as an event or course of events that will inevitably happen in the future. You have an awesome destiny to fulfill. Whether you fulfill your destiny is intricately related to your sense of identity and to how aware you are of your personal vision and purpose. An acute awareness of your personal vision and purpose provides you with an adequate perspective of time. And time is your most valuable commodity.

One of the wisest men in history, King Solomon, reminds us,

To everything there is a season and a time for every purpose under heaven.

Time is important because it is the medium through which you fulfill life's events. When you are conscious of your destiny, you realize that you were born for a specific time and that this is the only time available to you to manifest the greatness that rests inside of you.

In addition to equipping you to maximize your time, one goal of this work is to encourage you to pursue your passion and purpose and to realize that someone else's life could depend on you fulfilling your dream. That is why we so candidly share our deep struggles along with our successes. We want you to know for certain that because we fought to finish, you can too!

You could have been born during any period of time in history, but it is no coincidence that you are living at this particular moment in time. Even if your parents did not want you, you are here for a reason. If you have felt rejected, insignificant and useless yet never ceased searching for more from life, *now* is your time to learn how to experience a fulfilled life – a more excellent life than the one you knew before. All of your experiences make you uniquely you -- your parents, your family, your ethnicity, your personality, schooling, and the hosts of experiences, positive and negative, that make you, are all perfectly designed to propel you into your destiny.

Someone is waiting for you.

Who is suffering because you have not written the book? Who is ill because you have not found the cure? Who is impoverished because you have not developed the foundation? Who is ignorant because you are not their teacher? Which communities suffer because you are not there to advocate for them? How many audiences have been denied an escape from what ails them because they have yet to see your masterpiece, become lost in your dance, or carried away by your voice? The possibilities are endless. Living on purpose is critical because the hope that living with vision affords you enables you to live a life without limits.

You are full of potential! Think of yourself as a field of rich soil capable of producing innumerable crops. Despite the potential present the crops do not grow without the careful, specific, consistent attention of an individual skilled at making that particular crop grow. Similarly, in order for your soil, your life, to yield fruitful crops, you have to know what to do to get the most out of your life.

We wrote this book for you. It contains the "seeds" that you will need to aid you in producing a harvest for your life and your legacy.

One of the greatest laws of humanity is the law of sowing and reaping: *Whatsoever a man soweth that shall he reap.* Sometimes the law of sowing and reaping is interpreted as the law of cause and effect which says, "For every effect there is a cause." Achievement, influence, wealth, happiness, and prosperity are all direct and indirect results of specific causes or actions. Sir Isaac Newton captured the essence of the sowing and reaping principle when he explained, "For every action there is an equal and opposite reaction."

Each chapter in this workbook is full of "seeds" that, once applied, empower you to move closer to fulfilling your purpose and destiny. Revisit them often. Share them. Teach them.

Remember, a seed is a tiny beginning with a huge future. If you plant the "seeds" from this workbook into your life, water them, expose them to the proper amount of "light" (e.g., mentorship, reading, personal development, exercise, prayer, meditation, etc.) and allow them to germinate and take root (if you apply patience), you are guaranteed to experience success.

Will it be difficult? Yes, it will be very difficult at times, nonetheless, the difficulties you meet will resolve themselves as you advance. Proceed, and light will dawn, and shine with increasing clearness on your path.

Proceed.

Work. Love. Live. Be More Excellent!

Love,
Omar & Jéneen

MORE REVIEWS

In Don't Be Scared, Live on Purpose! Omar and Jéneen provide tangible tools to position you on the road to discovering your purpose and passion and to help you answer critical questions about your unique self. The overall flow of the book and the writing exercises allow you to dig deep into the well of your heart to discover how you should spend your time while you are here on earth.

I was convicted and challenged to live, work and love intentionally and I'm left feeling able and willing to take action in my life. The way Omar and Jéneen candidly share their stories, the experiences of others, and relevant quotes helped me gain a deeper understanding of the principles that were so strategically placed throughout this book. It was important for me to grasp these truths because not only is it transforming my life, I will be able to teach generations coming after me how to live on purpose. I ask myself, how different would many of our lives be if we would have learned these truths during childhood? But how exciting is it to know that we can now deposit these seeds into the next generation!

This book will touch your spirit, emotions and mind and cause you to want to take action. Beware -- you may shout out in excitement as Don't Be Scared. Live On Purpose! begins to shake and awaken you!

Adrianne Edwards
Single Mother Advocate
Abington, PA

This text by Omar M. Barlow and Jéneen Nicole Barlow, co-founders of BeMoreExcellent.com, obliterates complacency and compels the reader to seriously ponder, write and take action in order to discern the purpose of one's life. One is coached through an inward journey in search of life purpose without regards to fads or external opinions. The authors are confident that the treasure of life purpose exists within each of us, but, in fact, have been buried under layers of societal and cultural debris. The Barlows challenge the reader to listen to the voice within as it is compelled to speak through the use of provocative coaching questions and scenarios.

Questions are continually posed after much direct communication about such subjects as the necessity of asking questions and pushing oneself pass the fear of posing and responding to difficult inquiries. When answers come too glibly, one is to dive to a deeper level of asking. Every writing or question posed by the authors or the reader is a process of seeking understanding of oneself and others on the journey to uncover the specific life purpose within each of us. When purpose is encountered, The Barlows posit that the individual engages in 'Flow'—action and thought, insight and creativity, understanding and behavior are unified—they are one. The required depth of the Destiny process is seen in the five fundamental questions of life that the text boldly approaches: Who am I? Where did I come from? Why am I here? What can I do? Where am I going? Nothing is off-limits to examination in the pursuit of one's life purpose. The challenges of relationships, loneliness, fear, perceived inadequacies are explored in novel and real life settings so that they can also be viewed as assets instead of liabilities.

Time is our most precious commodity. Thus, to do the work of discerning one's destiny/purpose is to use wisely this most precious asset. Time effectively utilized to realize life purpose is the greatest of investments.

After reading about the experience of others as well as that of the authors, each chapter then directs the reader to respond in writing and subsequent action through the exercises offered. Again, questions abound but there is no sense of being abandoned by the writers. Always, there is the invitation to just seek The Barlows on their tweeter line. One does not glide through the text, but makes overnight stays in some chapters. Sometimes, one simply stops reading in order to ponder a concept, a story or a question. The pause is precipitated by the authors sometimes blatant, sometimes subtle challenge to consider in depth a statement, an inquiry, a narrative. The pause comes because life-debris may have been shifted by the exercises and a glimmer of life purpose has been exposed.

Don't Be Scared. Live On Purpose! is reader-friendly; however, the reader must use the most valuable commodity—time—to accomplish the goal of the text—the unearthing of one's life purpose. The text enables the attainment of this vital goal. Engagement with this text is a most profitable expenditure of one's time.

Dr. Cassandra W. Jones
CEO, Next Step Associates, LLCs
Bala Cynwyd, PA

I am a 37 year old female with one child. When I first began reading, Don't Be Scared. Live On Purpose! I assumed that this was going to be like any other self-help book that I have read. But it wasn't. From the first paragraph I could relate because at one point or another in my life I had these very same feelings, "I know that this is not the college major I should have chosen." Or I know that I deserve to earn a lot more money than this company will ever pay me." So that alone, had pulled me in and separated itself from the rest of the books on my shelf. The fact that the book touched on all bases: career, finances, love and family confirmed it completely for me because worrying about these things would have my brain in maximum power overdrive; keeping me up at night.

As the book began talking about a Destiny Statement™; I instantly began to self-reflect. However, as I reflected this time, I asked myself different questions. For example, "Do I fear challenging the status quo?" is a question in the book that I never considered or even gave a second thought. But in some instances, I have, especially when choosing my mate and my career, been afraid of that challenge. *Don't Be Scared. Live On*

Purpose! is definitely a page-turner and it is definitely a great investment. If you know in your heart that you need a change, but you are scared or unaware of how to begin making these changes, then this book is your next must read.

Kelley Worell Graduate Student
Philadelphia, PA

Don't Be Scared. Live on Purpose! adds to the body of valuable literature on what it means to live a purpose driven life, and is filled with practical things that we ought to consider in our daily approach in order to fully live up to our innate potential. The scope of this book involves a comparison of internal and external stories we can all relate, and combines biblical proverbs, alongside thought provoking quotes and micro narratives to help guide readers in understanding and applying essential pillars of purpose. Additionally, the book reminds us of the importance in asking thought provoking questions that are propelling and less prohibitive, which I personally found to be the most intriguing with where I am at in my personal journey.

There are numerous best-selling books that discuss why and even how to live a life of purpose;

however, this book carefully walks readers through concise and effective steps to begin a personalized process toward identifying, discussing, and placing the content into perspective that is guided while reading in order to articulate a clear personal mission and vision, captioned in the text as a "Destiny Statement™." We can easily interpret philosophy, but the world is full of dreamers, there are not enough who will move ahead and begin to take concrete steps to actualize their vision. This book facilitates the initial process with substance and tangible output.

I believe this book to be important for all individuals in today's society. Fact is, we live in a world of incessant cultural and economic change that has a core outcome, which demands we identify our x-factor and pursue a life of purpose. It is rare to see a point-by-point comparison between attributes described by people as contributing to success and others to failure.

While the content is in line with generally held beliefs about vision and mission statements, I was very interested in the conversation regarding the K-16 education system, found in the preface of the book. As an educator, I continuously observe how our education system fails many students in the sense that we manufacture young people who are smart and talented, yes; yet these very same young people are often anxious, timid, and for lack of better words lost, with little intellectual curiosity and a stunted sense of purpose, heading meekly in the same direction, great at what they are doing, but with a lost sense of why they are doing it. This book could actually be used in schools to provide students an opportunity to look beyond the surface and examine themselves, which would be the start to dismantling a systemic effect of our educational institutions. Similarly, this book could be greatly useful for adult professional development.

Overall, I would recommend this book as a foundational piece of literature for anyone interested in transforming his or her own trajectory. It also would be of interest for someone involved in transformational or organizational change, as people need to change their way of thinking to drive those at an organizational level. I consider it to be a good lead-in companion piece to other best-selling authors and resources cited in the book.

Armãndo R. Tolliver, Ed.D.
Secondary Education Practitioner
School District of Philadelphia
Philadelphia, PA

MORE EXCELLENT RESOURCES

Now that you have finished reading Don't ***Be Scared. Live on Purpose!*** *Volume I,* and you have a custom personal mission statement, you have a decision to make. Will you begin to take immediate action toward living out that mission or will you become complacent and stop here?

Omar and I want to help you maintain your momentum! To help you to take action we strongly suggest that you make the following resources a part of your personal and professional library. Do it today!

www.destinystatement.com

- **Free Four Pillars of Purpose Mp3**
- **Free Live on Purpose! Mission Statement Writing Guide**
- **Free Membership ~ Join the *Don't Be Scared. Live on Purpose!* Movement on Facebook Today**

Book The Barlows!

Request Omar, Jéneen, or both of The Barlows to keynote or train at your next conference or special event or to personally train/develop your staff or team.

Call 478.BARLOW2 now, visit **www.bemoreexcellent.com** or just send your request to: info@bemoreexcellent.com. Tell us what you need and we work with you to make it happen!

Visit The Barlows!

Visit **www.bemoreexcellent.com** to be the first to know what new resources and events Omar and Jéneen are offering to further assist you with Living on Purpose. An event's page and Jéneen's informational, inspirational *Be More Excellent Blog* are also there.

Twitter

Follow BE on Twitter: @BeMorExcellent

Facebook

Visit Omar and Jéneen online for daily inspiration and sure-fire strategies for manifesting your mission:

https://www.facebook.com/bemoreexcellent

Destiny Statement™ Executive Programs

Now let's get some tangible results so that you can truly live your dreams! Visit us now at:

www.destinystatement.com

Decide which Executive Program will most benefit you and take action.

- Apprentice Executive Program
- Aspiring Author's Program
- Virtual Destiny Statement Institute
- Custom Cash-Generating Curriculum™

For this purpose was I born, and for this cause came I into the world.

John 18:37

ꕥ

May you discover your purpose, and may you find the reason you came into the world.

Make it an excellent life!

Omar & Jéneen

43422865R00144

Made in the USA
Middletown, DE
09 May 2017